Proud to Be a Mammal

Czesław Miłosz was born in 1911 in the Lithuanian village of Šeteniai, then part of the Russian empire. He was educated at the Sigismund Augustus Gymnasium and Stefan Batory University in Vilnius, then part of Poland. He spent the Second World War in Warsaw in the Nazi-ruled 'General Government'. Working as the cultural attaché of the People's Republic of Poland, he defected to France in 1951. In 1960 Miłosz emigrated to the United States and ultimately became an American citizen. He taught for many years at the University of California, Berkley. In 1980 he was awarded the Nobel Prize for Literature. After the Cold War ended he divided his time between California and Poland. His major works include *The Captive Mind*, *The Issa Valley*, *Native Realm* and *Visions of San Francisco Bay*. His *New and Collected Poems, 1931-2001* and *To Begin Where I Am: Selected Essays* were both published in 2001. He died in Kraków in 2004.

CZESŁAW MIŁOSZ

Proud to Be a Mammal

Essays on War, Faith and Memory

Translated by Catherine Leach, Bogdana Carpenter and
Madeline G. Levine

PENGUIN BOOKS

PENGUIN CLASSICS

Published by the Penguin Group
Penguin Books Ltd, 80 Strand, London WC2R 0RL, England
Penguin Group (USA), Inc., 375 Hudson Street, New York, New York 10014, USA
Penguin Group (Canada), 90 Eglinton Avenue East, Suite 700, Toronto, Ontario, Canada M4P 2Y3
(a division of Pearson Penguin Canada Inc.)
Penguin Ireland, 25 St Stephen's Green, Dublin 2, Ireland (a division of Penguin Books Ltd)
Penguin Group (Australia), 250 Camberwell Road, Camberwell, Victoria 3124, Australia
(a division of Pearson Australia Group Pty Ltd)
Penguin Books India Pvt Ltd, 11 Community Centre, Panchsheel Park, New Delhi – 110 017, India
Penguin Group (NZ), 67 Apollo Drive, Rosedale, North Shore 0632, New Zealand
(a division of Pearson New Zealand Ltd)
Penguin Books (South Africa) (Pty) Ltd, 24 Sturdee Avenue, Rosebank, Johannesburg 2196, South Africa

Penguin Books Ltd, Registered Offices: 80 Strand, London WC2R 0RL, England

www.penguin.com

This collection is published with the kind permission of Farrar, Straus & Giroux in Penguin
Classics 2010

Native Realm first published 1968
To Begin Where I Am: Selected Essays first published 2001, translation copyright © Ferrar, Strauss
and Giroux, LLC
Proud to be a Mammal copyright © The Estate of Czesław Miłosz 2010
1

Copyright © Doubleday & Company and Czesław Miłosz 1968, 2001
Translation copyright © Catherine S. Leach, Bogdana Carpenter and Madeline G. Levine, 1968, 2001

All rights reserved

The moral right of the author and the translators has been asserted

Set in 10.5/13 pt Dante MT
Typeset by Ellipsis Books Limited, Glasgow
Printed in England by Clays Ltd, St Ives plc

978 – 0 – 141 – 19319 – 9

www.greenpenguin.co.uk

Mixed Sources
Product group from well-managed
forests and other controlled sources
www.fsc.org Cert no. SA-COC-1592
© 1996 Forest Stewardship Council

Penguin Books is committed to a sustainable future
for our business, our readers and our planet.
The book in your hands is made from paper
certified by the Forest Stewardship Council.

Contents

The Peace Boundary[*]

It is not my intention to write a commentary for Goya's drawings. The immensity of events calls for restraint, even dryness, and this is only fitting where words do not suffice. The thread of one man's destiny alone would be enough to ensnarl us in a hopeless tangle of individual and historical complexities. It would take an epic breadth to cope with them, but, most likely, broad panoramas of this era will be rare, since World War II was fought on a different scale than, say, the Napoleonic Wars; and, besides, the demands placed on a writer by the development of sociology and psychology, are now much greater. Yet

* In 1939, both Nazi and Soviet propaganda used the high-sounding term 'peace boundary' when speaking of the line, known in history as the Molotov-Ribbentrop line, agreed upon by the two powers (in a secret protocol of the non-aggression pact signed August 23) to demarcate German and Soviet areas of influence in Poland. Needless to say, its use here is ironic. (Tr.)

if I were to present a personal story with a purely subjective slant, I would solve nothing because I would be leaving out the most interesting part. Again, I must repeat here that this is not a diary; I am not telling what happened to me from day to day or from month to month. To do so I would have to recreate certain hazy states of mind that are still not clear to me. I shall limit myself, therefore, to a few scenes as if I were working with scissors and miles of film footage. The frames I cut should be intelligible to a wider audience, not just to fanciers of Expressionism.

When the blitzkrieg began, I felt a need to carry out orders of some sort, and thus to relieve myself of responsibility. Unfortunately, it was not easy to find someone to give orders. But very soon I was wearing something like a uniform made up of ill-matching pieces, unable, however, to revel in any more glorious deeds than taking part in the retreat. The shock of disaster followed immediately. Yet for me that September of 1939 was a breakthrough, which must be hard to imagine for anyone who has never lived through a sudden collapse of the whole structure of collective life. In France, the blitzkrieg did not have the same effect.

I could reduce all that happened to me then to a few things. Lying in the field near a highway bombarded by airplanes, I riveted my eyes on a stone and two blades of grass in front of me. Listening to the whistle of a bomb, I suddenly understood the value of matter: that stone and those two blades of grass formed a whole kingdom, an infinity of forms, shades, textures, lights. They were the universe. I had always refused to accept the division into macro- and micro-cosmos; I preferred to contemplate a piece of bark or a bird's wing rather than sunsets or sunrises. But now I saw into the depths of matter with exceptional intensity.

Something else was the mixture of fury and relief I felt when I realized that nothing was left of the ministries, offices, and Army. I slept a deep sleep in the hay barns along the way. The nonsense was over at last. That long-dreaded fulfillment had freed us from the self-reassuring lies, illusions, subterfuges; the opaque had become transparent; only a village well, the roof of a hut, or a plow were real, not the speeches of statesmen recalled now with ferocious irony. The land was singularly naked, as it can only be for people without a state, torn from the safety of their habits.

Regardless of the words I exchanged with the people in whose company I found myself escaping toward the East, I already saw the future differently than they. No one in Poland, neither then nor later, believed in Hitler's ultimate victory. Characteristic of

Poles is the strong conviction that God intervenes personally in the affairs of history to side with the just, and therefore evil is doomed to failure. Armed with such a conviction, the Poles had many a time thrown themselves into hopeless struggles and were subsequently surprised when God did not help them and they lost after all – although this did not shake their belief in a final triumph. I, too, dismissed the probability of a German millennium, but semi-consciously my mind worked differently. There was too much of the Manichaean in me to accept the thought that the divine finger would insert itself into the iron necessity of the world's course.

What mainly set me apart from my traveling companions, however, was that they were unaware of either the scope of the tragedy or its durable effects. They placed their hopes in France, a consolation to which I, with my year in Paris behind me, responded as to a fairy tale. The only ones who completely grasped what had happened were the Communists (including the Trotskyites), but they were thrown into an embarrassing situation by the Red Army's friendly meeting with the German Army and by the dividing up of Poland's corpse. Whenever I came across any of them, we recognized each other by our jeering attitude toward our environment, which was not unlike the way sober people treat pathetically gibbering drunks.

But our sobriety was relative. It did not go beyond a feeling for the proportions of the cataclysm. The Communists were bolstered by a variant of the belief in Providence; that is, in the fundamental and hidden rationality of the historical process, which could not possibly be on the side of the Nazis. To a certain point I admitted the validity of their arguments, especially when they appealed to the dialectic of the world: too sly to be overpowered by the blind and stupid force of the sword. But how and when revenge would come no one dared to prophesy. Doubtless the key was to be sought in Russia. Contact with that country, however, was so painful that several Communists even escaped from the Soviet to the German zone. My lucidity, which in the beginning had produced relief, soon gave way to a torpor or malignant fever, and for several months I was tossed about by fantastic circumstances, as if my will had fled. I shall pass over those adventures because to describe them would require an entirely different language than is used in this book.

If at the beginning of 1940 I found myself once again in my home town, I must ascribe that both to circumstances and to a dark instinct. It acted like a doctor amid a universal rupture of all ties, and advised me to recover my bond with my family and my native

Czesław Miłosz

region. Wilno, like all of Poland's eastern territory, was occupied by the Red Army after the defeat, and a few weeks later was ceded to Lithuania in token of friendship. The friendship was not exactly disinterested: Lithuania, like Latvia and Estonia, had to accept Soviet military bases. Nevertheless, the three tiny countries owed their independence to the cautious game between two giants, and their three governments dodged desperately about to avoid embittering either Germany or Russia. The prewar era was still alive here – normally stocked stores, restaurants, coffeehouses, punctual trains. In Wilno, newspapers in various languages, including Polish, appeared, though not without a struggle with the censor's office. It was hard for me to recognize that dreamlike city – not only because a different flag was flying on the castle ramparts and the names of streets and signs had been changed. Crowds of Polish refugees, whom Lithuania received hospitably even though she dreaded a grimace from her powerful neighbors, had turned the city into a feverish tower of Babel. There was a flourishing trade in currency and passports, contagious gossip, waves of panic, overflowing post offices where heads of rabbinical schools, officers of the defeated army, diplomats without assignments, and all those with relatives and friends abroad were sending off telegrams to France, England, and America. Departures by plane via Stockholm were becoming more and more difficult. New refugees flowed in constantly, risking, in the case of capture at the border, a trip to Stalin's concentration camps. Once they reached that desired island of safety, they quickly realized that the island was a sinking floe and escape had been cut off.

The Hotel Europa was typically situated for our town. It stood at the intersection of the two most colorful streets: Dominican Street boasted mainly Catholic churches and monasteries, while German Street had, ever since the Middle Ages, served as the main artery through the Jewish district. It was here that Felix and his wife lived. The disasters I had been living through drew me to the court that surrounded this man; so it will be in place if I sketch his portrait here.

Felix resembled a Japanese, with his black hair, sallow complexion, and filigreed refinement; he was always impeccable, elegant, and fragrant with cologne. He came from a Jewish family so rich that he had, it seems, no occupation, although he had completed his technical studies in Belgium. Just before the outbreak of the war, he sold his apartment houses in Warsaw and went into exile with a large suitcase loaded with dollars and gold. He also took his young, attractive wife, together with her furs and jewels. Their relationship was built on alternate scenes of hatred and tender reconciliation. His wife, profiting from her physical superiority, would beat him or, if he put up resistance, would threaten to commit suicide and run toward the window. Felix then fled and shut himself up in the bathroom – not to see. A few minutes later, friends (who usually played the role of arbiters) would knock on the door of the bathroom, from which a weak voice came: 'Well? Did she jump?'

Felix was an inveterate alcoholic but he did not like to drink alone. Quite the contrary, he constantly needed a choir around him to tell fairy tales, anecdotes, and jokes, which would make his existence pleasant. He appreciated intellectual refinement, hence his attraction to artists and poets; these found in him a perfect teat – that is, a man who graciously allowed himself to be milked. Since many of them had wandered hither from Warsaw, he soon gathered an impressive court and his feasts drew a few dozen people.

The drinking usually began at eleven in the morning. As the day advanced, however, it did not take on an extreme form. The poets J. and S., who set the pace, were too much the seasoned drunkards to fall into oblivion. They sipped vodka from large tumblers, continually refilling them to the brim, and carried on a ceaseless palaver throughout the entire day and far into the night. Next morning the hangover had to be cured, so the whole thing started all over again. Thus time, meaningless and hopeless, was experienced differently than in naked reality; it was transformed by alcohol.

Our gatherings were an uninterrupted 'feast during the plague,' and those assembled knew full well that death stalked beyond the doors and had to be out-witted. That company suited me because it lived without illusions, practicing a macabre humor and laughing, while that was still possible, at the bloody comedy of the two empires that surrounded us. S., for example, lectured on his theories of Hitler: the Führer was only playing the fool for his nation's benefit; after screaming himself to death he threw off his uniform with disgust, put on English flannels, smoked English cigarettes, drank whiskey, and expressed the highest contempt for Germany. The war between the Soviet Union and Finland also gave S. the opportunity to tell many stories, such as the one about the adventures of a Soviet soldier who took a wall clock, the largest wristwatch he had ever seen, from a Finnish hut and carried it around in his knapsack, bent double under the weight. Felix listened greedily to the anecdotes and limericks that we thought up under the influence of vodka. He could veil over his fear with them, but most likely he had always feared existence.

I could not relax. When one is in a state of exceptional nervous tension, alcohol has little effect and neither unsteadiness nor vomiting disrupt the precise functioning of the brain. Objects seemed to wound me as if they sent out sharp rays piercing the skin, and I hurried down the street with averted eyes, desiring only to be seated at Felix's table as quickly as possible; there, past and future were at least partly obliterated. I could not read, I could not write, nor could I participate in discussions that were mocked by events. I could only, and unsuccessfully at that, try to regain some sort of quiet, either vegetative or animal.

My new companions took refuge in subjective time through fornication, which both men and women considered an effective way of forgetting. But not all were satisfied with the ordinary forms of that activity; they searched for newer varieties. For instance, J. said to me that doing it in church was very pleasant. I guessed his motives: sexuality must be seasoned with evil; if all taboos vanish and there is nothing to break, it loses its appeal. J. was bored with the natural; he desired a prohibition, something to give mystery to sex to make it worthwhile. Looking at his partner, a slender girl with a tendency to blush, I imagined how she yielded to his advances somewhere in the empty nave of a church, modestly lowering her doe's lashes. I, for several reasons, observed a strict purity. What inclined me to that was my faithfulness to a close person who had remained in Warsaw and my somewhat magic view of the connection between all things: the sexual act was equal to saying yes to the world. The precarious safety, the dangers ahead, called for preparedness. I felt that fate was not to be tempted by pretending to accept the present. Besides, in moments of personal difficulty I usually feared sexual freedom as something that must draw down vengeance, since it leads to a forbidden release of energy. So I deliberately cultivated an unbearable nervous tension and mitigated it only with vodka.

The sudden death of one of our companions, the poet S., occurred in circumstances that suited quite well the phantasmagoria we upheld. It also suited S.'s macabre mind. S. was thirty. He died *in coitu* as a result of an injection that a certain rich lady, and a rather pitiless hussy, had herself given him in bed. When we visited him at the morgue in St. Jacob's Church, where an autopsy was performed to establish the cause of death, we were moved by the beauty and harmony of his features, whose defects, arising from a thyroid condition, had completely vanished. Afterward, we all accompanied him across town, walking in the huge funeral procession. His name was known to all readers of the Polish press, and he was given a splendid funeral.

City cemeteries are usually gloomy patches of stony space, but not in Wilno. Rosa Cemetery, where we had chosen a plot for him – not far from the grave of a nineteenth-century poet, Syrokomla – spreads over steep hillsides overgrown with ancient trees. Here, on All Souls' Day, thousands of candles and oil lamps are lit on the graves; they burn and flicker in the wind through the branches on the slopes above and in the ravines below. And here, under a large basalt stone, lies the heart of Piłsudski, the creator of between-the-wars Poland. We had done what we could for S., thinking all the while that maybe he had not met the worst fate. Then we began the funeral repast, drawing up a chair for his ghost, in front of which one had the urge to place a filled glass.

It would be easy to call us all degenerate. We were, however, people of the most diverse kind, drawn together by accident. In effect, there was a certain wisdom in our behavior, stemming from the awareness that in some traps it is better to behave passively than to frustrate oneself with sterile thrashing around. Felix, by selling his goods and spending his gold on the pleasures of entertaining, was bearing testimony to his superiority over those who clutched at their already useless wealth. His drunken gatherings were lighthearted, in keeping with the morrow that would demand nonchalance and the casting off of every burden. They were a farewell to the historical phase that was passing away forever in this part of the world.

The summer of 1940 arrived, and I witnessed the end of Lithuania. Poland had gone down amid flames and uproar; here not a single shot was fired. The German Armies were just then entering Paris. In the coffeehouse on Cathedral Square, I lazily contemplated a streak of sunshine on the table and the print dresses of the women who passed by the window; many of them had arrived here with only the knotted bundles of runaways. Already they had managed to purchase things, taking advantage of the well-stocked stores where you did not have to use ration cards or stand in lines. A sudden heavy scrape of metal on the pavement roused my curiosity, as it did everybody's. People got up from their tables only to freeze in their tracks as they watched the large, dusty tanks with their little turrets from which Soviet officers waved amicably. To connect in one's mind what could have passed for a simple military exercise with the hard fact of occupation demanded an inhuman effort, as one can imagine, when beautiful weather, newspaper kiosks, flower stands, and a little dog sprinkling the trunk of a linden tree, make it seem incredible that the decisions of unknown politicians can disturb the normal run of things.

To the uninitiated observer, nothing special happened that day. Only toward evening, megaphones began to blare and patrols of Asiatic soldiers paced up and down, their thin bayonets, like awls drawn out to a thread, sticking up three feet above their heads. But the population, thanks to the proximity of the Polish counties that had already been occupied, was initiated – except for a few hundred naive Communist enthusiasts. The fear, as it mounted from hour to hour, seemed to become almost a physical, tangible presence.

I went down to the river, sat on a bench, and watched the suntanned boys in their kayaks, the revolving rod of a tiny steamboat's engine, the colored boats, which you rowed standing at the back, using one long oar. I was sorry for my city because I knew every stone of it; I knew the roads, forests, lakes, and villages of this country whose people and whose landscapes had been thrown like grist into a mill. I experienced nothing of this sort when Hitler conquered Poland because in my heart I could not regard National Socialism as a durable phenomenon. A wolf is no doubt a dangerous animal, and should he bite, consolation is no help;

yet together with the image of his fangs and claws another image rises within us: of automatic weapons, of tanks, of planes, against which the wolf is power-less. For me the Revolution and Marxism were the equivalent of this higher technology. National Socialism was too pure an evil, and it had already, at least in theory, yielded to Lenin's more diabolical sheaf of both good and evil. My thinking, of course, was not that cold. It was simply that the sandbars in front of the electric-power station where children were standing with fishing poles, the river current, the sky, all spoke to me of an irrevocable sentence.

In the days that followed I noticed that many people, who had up to then passed me indifferently in the street, now bowed to me with smiles of the sincerest friendship. Because I had the reputation of being a Communist, they calculated on my being powerful, and now was the time to win my favor. Doubtless one should have written a few enthusiastic poems in honor of the imminent annexation of the Baltic countries, by means of 'elections,' to the Soviet Union. Those bows gave me much malevolent pleasure, although the sense of power they afforded was not of a kind these foresighted individuals imagined. I concealed my plan to play a better joke on them.

Politically I was closest to a small group of Polish Socialists who had maintained contact with Stockholm from formerly neutral Lithuania – Swedish Socialists lent effective help in passing on conspiratorial material – and with America, where their ideological comrade, Oscar Lange, was lecturing at the University of Chicago. That Lange was later on to become the first Ambassador of People's Poland in the United States was one of the surprises of the usual political *contredanse* performed in stormy times by various public figures. It was in that group that I met Sophia.

Sophia could have been fifty or sixty, she was black-haired (dyed), intelligent, vehement, and smoked like a chimney, tearing her cigarettes in half for economy's sake and stuffing them into a glass cigarette holder. As a liaison carrying money and documents she had already made two illegal trips between Wilno and Warsaw. Without further ado we came to an agreement to set off together the next time, and not to wait long since the journey would be difficult and the border was 'hardening.'

Our protracted discussions over the map will go uncelebrated by those who cannot appreciate the peculiar talent, which all totalitarian states seem to have, for multiplying barbed-wire barriers along boundary lines. The simplest thing would have been to go straight to East Prussia; there, however, without knowing the terrain and without being able to pass for local residents, we would be easy prey for the

Nazis. The only advisable thing was to head for a Polish county wedged between Lithuania and East Prussia, which was part of the territory annexed to the Reich. If we managed to get across the Russian-German border successfully (knock on wood), then on the other side of that county we would catch up with the old boundary (still patrolled) between Poland and East Prussia. From there we would push our way across East Prussia to her southwestern edge, where we would force our third border into the Polish counties that were now also part of the Reich. Our fourth and last border-crossing would bring us into the German protectorate, with the cities Warsaw and Cracow; that is, into the Government-General. The reason for these rather insane obstacles raised by the Nazis within an occupied country was quite clear: it was a question of immobilizing the skittish human animal, of cutting off his possibilities of escape from one place to another in the face of danger.

It would be a lie if I were to claim that I made my choice as one looks at two sides of a scale, measuring the pros and cons. Had I begun to think in this way I would have probably undertaken no decision at all, because my imagination would have reminded me of the people I had known who had been caught trying to cross the borders and who had been sucked into the great funnel of jails or camps in the north. I was aided by vanity, or pride, which showed in the contemptuous curl of my lips: who are these people anyway, I said to myself; why should they deal with me as they please and assume that everyone will bend to their wishes because they have power? For personal reasons I had long had the intention of going to Warsaw, so why should I defer to necessity now and condemn myself to life imprisonment within a system that, who knows, might never fall? Besides, the passivity and the nascent servility around me demanded some kind of deed in order to break the spell; and after my long vegetation at Felix's court, I could take no more idleness without aim or achievement. What would have happened had they shoved a piece of paper at me and ordered: Either write a political ode or spend five years in camp? But I refused to admit a single thought of failure as I planned my flight.

The preparations took time and required complete secrecy; we could not betray ourselves to anyone, and had to pretend we were overjoyed by the new order. I took part in the 'elections'; that is, my face wore a serious expression when I dropped my card into the ballot box, having written something on it in pencil that I shall keep to myself as a voter's privilege. The result – ninety-nine per cent for a single slate – had been foreclosed, like the unanimous demand for Lithuania's annexation to the Soviet Union.

Nor could I say goodbye to my friends because the gossip would have made the rounds of every coffee-house in half an hour. So I did not say goodbye to Felix. I shall have to recreate his subsequent adventures from the accounts I heard later on. Felix was scared. One night a crony of his, the lawyer X., first persuaded, then helped him to bury his treasure in the garden. Anxiety, however, seized Felix the next morning. He was worried about whether the place had been well chosen. That night the two of them again went out with shovels, but found nothing. It could only have been sheer coincidence that the lawyer, from that moment on, swam in money, while Felix's drinking companions had to pass the hat to buy a train ticket to Manchuria for him and his wife. Felix's departure bordered on a miracle, since the authorities granted rights of transit only to the possessors of Japanese visas at a time when it was already impossible to obtain such a visa.

It seems that a certain foresighted Rabbi helped them out of the fix: in his unfathomable wisdom he had collected absolutely all possible visas (even unnecessary ones) while all the consulates had still been operating. The Japanese visa, which the experts had copied from his passport, sold for a high fee, but it was marked by one defect: no one in the city knew the Japanese alphabet, and therefore could not have guessed that each visa contained the name of its first owner. When the five-hundredth Silberstein passed over the Manchurian frontier, the Japanese began to worry. Whether the story is true or merely an anecdote, Felix, at any rate, made it to Shanghai and from there to Australia. He enlisted in the American Army and perished in an auto accident in Hawaii. I shall do no discredit to his memory, perhaps, if I make the conjecture that he died in an unsober condition.

Sophia irritated me when she announced, two days before we were to leave, that guides cost a great deal and we did not have enough money; she suggested we take a third partner, who, in exchange for the privilege, would finance our expedition. He was a pharmacist, driven to Wilno by the war, who dreamed of returning to his family. Would I agree? There was something strange in her tone of voice. Either the candidate was offering her an exceptionally large sum and she was arranging a deal on the side, or she was foreseeing that he would get us into trouble. Somehow the sweetness in her voice was too unlike her. I tried to object: in that case our two passes are worthless, because there is not enough time to make a third. I had obtained those German passes, which guaranteed transit from the little town of Suwałki in the Reich, via East Prussia to the Government-General, with great difficulty. Produced by a local printing press, they were counterfeit from start to finish, including the magnificent seals with the swastika – those seals proved that our university's Fine Arts Department was training skillful artists. Actually the passes did not guarantee anything, but still . . . Sophia's proposal meant that not one border but four would have to be crossed on foot. Naturally, she argued that we risked even more with my uncertain passes. Finally I succumbed to the mathematical argument, when she set down the cost in figures on a scrap of paper.

The first time I set eyes on our third man was the morning of our departure at the railroad station. I saw immediately what had caused Sophia's strange expression. Sophia, in a kerchief and carrying an old knapsack, looked like a country schoolteacher, nor did I, with my homespun bag and the face of a native, stand out. But the pharmacist – a grayish, bloated face, faded-blue little eyes sneaking fearful and suspicious glances in our direction. The sluggishness of a hippopotamus, the very caricature of a bourgeois. He was dragging a huge suitcase tied round with a leather strap.

The landscapes of my childhood rolled by beyond the train window, and quickly, but more strongly than if I had deliberately brought it to mind, the name of a station forever linked in my memory with a true and tragic love of my boyhood years leaped out before my eyes and passed. Above all, however, I was aware of the man across from me, or, more precisely, of my own wounded self-esteem. After we had exchanged several remarks, I decided he was a pig and a pitiful fool. Was such a one as he, then, to be my comrade in action – an action that was more or less equal to a manifesto of independence? Was it not a punishment to humiliate me? There was I, an intellectual who might have stayed on with unhappy but at least thinking beings, and I had to escape with him, a know-nothing, doomed by history for caring only about his stinking money and family bedding. Over there, I thought to myself, west of the line guarded by the two armies, history's sentence will catch up with him, in a different way, perhaps, but it will. At this decisive moment, which has been ripening for so long, when there is nothing in Europe but Hitlerism and Stalinism, when one must declare oneself for either one or the other, I am only deluding myself with the hope of an indeterminate third solution because I am unable to base it on anything. On anything except my disgust – and then to be disgusted by this fellow here! If we are caught, this man will be my cellmate, my neighbor.

Our departure had been timed so that we would arrive in the afternoon of a market day, when it was easier to get lost in the crowd. The name of the town was more Catholic than Lithuanian: Kalvaria. We had a 'contact' there – a local farmer. Among the flour sacks in his barn we listened to his review of the situation. The border at village X was impossible, village Y too; one could try near village Z. That cart in the yard (unharnessed horses were munching in their feedbags near it) had just come from there and we could ride back in it, but it would pick us up half a mile outside of town because the NKVD patrols were stationed at all the exit thoroughfares and were checking documents. We readied ourselves, and within a few hours, at a given signal, we began to steal through orchards, hedges, carrot fields, and cabbages. I carried the pharmacist's suitcase because after the first few minutes he was already panting and out of breath. Drenched in sweat, I cursed the idiotic predicament that had turned all my smuggler's shrewdness to no use; if such a cavalcade, with that suitcase, were spotted by an informer even from a distance, it would have meant the end. The idiocy dragged on as we trudged over the sandy road that led toward the border. Our cart was moving along close by, but for the moment pretending it had nothing to do with us.

As soon as I was lying on my back in the hay at the bottom of the cart, gazing up at the sky overhead, where clouds, rosy from the setting sun, floated lazily, I felt the inner calm that had eluded me for so many months. No conflicts, no hesitations, no fear even –

fear was only in my nerves, it did not penetrate further. My mind was disconnected, it did not disturb my inner harmony. I listened to the voice of my organism: my body believed deeply in Providence and submitted in advance to its decrees; whatever happens to me has been destined to happen, so why be troubled? To this day I wonder to what extent that voice in other people signifies an acceptance of everything, and to what extent it is untrustworthy. It helped me to control the pounding of my heart so that, as we passed the NKVD camp in a forest glade, I phlegmatically chewed on a blade of grass. Beria's soldiers, who looked like rough-hewn stones in their long military coats, were lined up in rows, singing.

Here the terrain changed from flatland to country-side. The road wound through a ravine, through groves of pine and alder, over hill and dale, through orchards, then we were in the village. We pulled up in front of a hut, were quickly hustled into a dark entrance, then ordered in a whisper to climb up to the loft and pull the ladder after us.

Those forty-eight hours we spent in the hayloft could have supplied the material for a theater play with a cast of three. We were forbidden to speak out loud, to knock, to rustle the hay. Because there was no window, the roof was our only observation point; from time to time, peering through it with one eye, we saw the point of a bayonet carried by the NKVD soldier patrolling the village street. Sophia unburdened her ire by taking it out on the pharmacist. Nothing, perhaps, can equal the cruelty of a woman if she despises a male. For that matter, the pharmacist's every gesture, his every word, his very person even, was provoking. He drooled with terror and infected us with his fear; he did and undid his leather money-belt that was stuffed with dollars, turning his back lest, accidentally, we were to count his wealth; he treated us like two hoodlums from the underground to whom he had entrusted his valuable life; he did not know how to walk or even how to eat bread and sausage quietly; he did not know how to take care of his other needs either. Sophia squatted discreetly in a corner, I hid behind a rafter. The pharmacist restrained himself and suffered until suddenly, right in front of us, he undid his trousers, took out his member, as wrinkled as an elephant's trunk, and poured forth, bleating with pleasure, completely indifferent to everything save the relief of emptying his bladder. Sophia observed this unblinkingly, then turned away and said: 'Slob!' The name stuck.

Since we spoke little, she ostracized him from our society by a terrorism of silence. My cautious attempts to appease her or to make her realize that Slob, too, was a human being did not come from love of my neighbor but from my sense of outrage at the earth, as an exceptionally terrifying place: if even the goodness of women is an illusion and what they really value in us are only cavemen virtues; i.e., strength, efficiency, energy. My calm, and my enterprising spirit, though they had earned me Sophia's friendship, were not qualities with which I hoped to merit the warm feelings of others. They ebbed and flowed independently of my will, and who knows, if Sophia were to meet me in another chapter of my life, whether I would not become an object of her ridicule? I mentally arraigned her in an antifeminist court, and felt a tinge of contempt for the low urges that had crept out from under the surface of her so-called culture. My thirst for justice, however, came to naught. Because whenever I showed Slob the least sympathy, he began to whine and snivel and, worse still, mistook my gesture for evidence of solidarity with him against Sophia. Complete wretchedness compounded with complete lack of tact.

This seething behind closed doors was interrupted now and then by sounds from below, none too agreeable for our over-stimulated nerves. When our farmer cleared his throat in the agreed way, we let down the ladder and he climbed up to us for a council of war. His talk was better than a map – much more detailed than anything we had. The village stood on a high bank over the marshes; that is, over the basin of a semidrained, postglacial lake. The end of the low ground was already on the German side. 'In spring and autumn the water gets pre-e-e-etty high – boy oh boy, the Jews that drowned here running from Hitler! But you can get across now.' Guards keep watch on the shore. Of Russian talents he had the highest opinion: 'They are real woodsmen.' He told us that they go out in fives, sit down in the grass, and, after a rest, move on further; a naive person would assume that no one remained behind, but they have just relieved their comrades who were hidden there, leaving two from their group and taking two. We should wait until Sunday night, when there will be dancing in the village. The girls promised to help. They would keep the soldiers talking or do something to distract the guard at the entrance to the marshes – he was the most dangerous.

Even before the war this village had derived much of its income from contraband; then, however, neither Polish nor Lithuanian guards were known for their alertness, and even if one fell into their hands it meant, at the most, no more than the loss of one's goods or a few months' arrest. That evening we were joined by two young boys, already seasoned professionals. They had scarcely opened the door of the cottage, taking care that it did not creak, when they broke into a run, and we after them, with Slob wheezing excruciatingly. In one sprint we reached the path to the bottom of the ravine. Our guides often stopped to listen here, and with good reason, for at every turn I was startled by the sight of strange statues standing in front of us: these were irregular, glacial rock formations, tall and bright in the moonlight and casting black blotches of shadows. From afar they looked like people; close up they were no less fearsome, because a man could have been hidden behind each of them. When water at last began to slosh over our shoes, I drew my breath with relish, savoring the smell of osiers, marsh rosemary, and wet moss, the smell of my native land.

I felt at home in such swamps, and I have always been affected by their somewhat melancholy beauty. The smooth sheet of water shone with an oily gleam between clumps of vegetation, and here and there on it a motionless piece of dry leaf floated. We broke into it and sank up to our knees, then up to our thighs. Slob still strained our tempers because he splashed, caught himself on bushes, and fell behind, forcing us to go back and pull him out of the brambles. When the water reached our waists, he managed to fall in up to his neck or go under, calling out in a hoarse gurgle for help. In the moonlight I caught a glimpse of his exhausted, inhumanly mud-smeared face.

Sophia preserved her sense of humor. In a mutual effort, we rescued her from a treacherous quagmire where she had sunk up to her shoulders and was afraid to move for fear the mud would suck her in. Almost naked in her clinging dress, she smiled: 'I lost my panties!'

Once a signal of alarm stopped us: only the hiss of air bubbles from the peat we had trampled . . . but then the sound of heavy, splashing steps. They did not sound too far away. A while later, though, our guides said: 'Beast!' A moose or a deer was coming from East Prussia. He could be happy because for him every man was a danger; he did not have to worry about changes of governments or systems.

Those few miles we had to wade through took us many hours. The stars were growing pale and dawn was already blowing in the air when we stood on dry ground. We, vague shadows between the white birch trunks, were in Hitler's state. Around us the loose rustle of leaves, the fairyland of a midsummer night's dream, and within me the triumph and strength that comes of victory in spite of all obstacles. I was struck by the weirdness of the scene: at a time when Oberon's horn should be sounding in the forest and Titania awakening from the spell Puck had cast on her, our guides, lying on the moss, were diligently counting their dollars. After being taken to a friendly hut in the first village, we made at once for the hayloft and fell asleep on the spot.

The peasant cart rattled along the highway under a fine rain. Our route took us from the north to the south of this country of windswept highlands, lakes, and spruce forests that were familiar to me from before the war. Just before the little town of Suwałki, our driver turned down a road that cut through the fields and around the vegetable gardens until we reached a side street where he stopped in front of a small one-story wooden house. The fullness of being human is difficult to achieve; but to this day the inhabitants of that little house, a young droshky driver and his wife, who was suckling an infant, are proof to me that it is possible. Their fear struggled with their sense of duty toward their neighbor, and it was precisely the obviousness of their inner battle – although they tried to hide it, showing us brotherly kindness – that clothed their persons in a special pathos.

I exposed them and myself to danger by going out for a walk around the town. But in the course of that half hour I grasped the essence of the Nazi régime. My footsteps echoed in the empty streets; I met a few old women. All the Jews had been murdered or jailed, and the huge army garrison that had stood here before the war no longer existed. At first I attributed the depopulation to that, but then the funereal black banner of the S.S. and my visit to the pharmacy explained the real reason. There behind the counter, dressed in a white coat, stood a boy whom I recognized as the owner's son. When he saw me his face turned ashen and he began signalling with his hands not to come nearer, as if he were seeing a ghost. I did come nearer however, and the boy, trembling, threw me a few words. I returned, restraining my speed with a nonchalant swing, trying to act as if I *had a right* to my liberty. The entire male population of the area, with a few exceptions, had been deported to forced-labor or concentration camps. The rains still had not washed away the bloody patches left behind from the mass executions on the towns' squares. As I found out later my fifteen-year-old cousin, a resident of that part of Poland, found himself, more or less around that time, behind barbed wire in the camp at Oranienburg-Sachsenhausen. Two years later he was dead.

We would have to risk taking the train to the station at the East Prussian border. One must keep in mind that to the south lay Russian-occupied territory; therefore there was no other way. At dawn our droshky driver took us to the railroad station. We shivered both from cold and from fear, which the empty platform hardly allayed. Our next 'contact' – the restaurant in a border village – turned out to be a good one. We were received hospitably and told that documents were examined aboard the train, on the Prussian side, but that we could avoid it by paying; a messenger was also dispatched to arrange for it. At night we crawled over pasturelands, under wire fences, bumping into cows in the dark. A Polish farmhand, doing forced labor for a German *Bauer*, was waiting for us at an agreed spot in a buggy harnessed with a pair of strong horses. He chose back roads to avoid the highways; after some twenty miles we arrived at the third or fourth station on the line, just in time for the morning train.

While riding in the train through East Prussia, we did not speak to each other in order not to call attention to ourselves. I had time then to think about the little painted houses, the cleanliness, the order. Terror and destruction were for export, not for home use; on the contrary, they served to enrich one's home country. Wretched humanity beyond one's own frontiers was simply material to be cut and shaped as one pleased. I sorted the stories that the young farmhand had not grudged us during our night ride. Almost all the farms here had been allotted Polish prisoners of war or deportees for forced labor, and the luck of the Poles varied according to the kind of master they received. I was able to guess from a few details that our driver's liberty to use the horses for purposes not of the most loyal sort derived from his status with the *Bauer*'s wife. He had assumed all the rights and duties of her former husband, who – ironic vengeance of destiny – had perished on the front in the Polish campaign. But the young Pole hated with a quiet peasant hatred – like all his countrymen here he had to wear the letter 'P' sewn on his sleeve – and he had already singled out a farm to grab as soon as the war was over. His belief in victory, that summer of 1940 at the apogee of Hitler's power, was inflexible and irrational. East Prussia would fall to Poland: that was that.

Trouble awaited us in Ortelsburg. The next cross-over point, Sophia confessed to me, had a bad name: be careful, there was something fishy. Since Slob was about as much help as excess baggage, Sophia and I dropped into a smoke-filled little dive to rack our brains over a beer. Somehow we were going to have to find out from someone how to get to the border villages; but we could not trust any Germans. I latched onto a little man with a red nose, a Mazurian in a railroad employee's uniform, and began to pour cognac into him. His usefulness added up to zero because he slipped at once into an alcoholic stupor. Yet I rank him as one of the enigmatic wise men. While staring numbly at the table, he would repeat stubbornly every so often: 'The Russkies will come.' In that tippler dwelled a powerful, skeptical mind. Immune to official propaganda, he had come to his own conclusions, based on some sort of personal observations and intuitions, which were highly offensive to the German millennium.

Since we were getting nowhere, I decided to make a last attempt – which testifies to my instinctual attachment to the Catholic Church as a supranational institution, or at least to my opinion of its servants as people who relatively seldom serve Caesar: to seek help from the parish priest. Of course I knew, as I inquired about the address of the rectory, that I was taking a chance, but sometimes chance just needs a little help. As soon as I had opened the door, my foolishness overwhelmed me. A double chin above a starched collar, fair-haired heads of children, a catechism lesson, his eyes and the children's reflecting surprise and dread at the sight of a dirty, stammering Polish bandit. In half a minute the Church as a supranational institution fell to pieces. I closed the door and walked down the street whistling.

We abandoned our search and took the train to Willenberg, the last station on the southern border of East Prussia. There my stubborn insistence on having counterfeit passes made in Wilno proved not to have been in vain. Sophia had wandered off somewhere, and Slob and I were waiting for her when suddenly a gendarme loomed in front of us and asked to see our documents. I gave him my pass while Slob cringed, almost shrank out of sight, pretending to wrestle with the strings of his knapsack. Our Wilno artists knew their craft, for the big fellow in the green uniform merely waved his hand: never mind, it was O.K.

Then we had a hard time renting horses to get to an out-of-the-way village named Kleine Leschinen. Forest and more forest, then the lonesome house of a rich *Bauer*. He was a Mazurian called Deptuła. He did not invite us in but ordered us to wait in the nearby oak grove until sundown, and he would send us a boy guide. The sun was setting, the birds sang with flutelike sweetness, and I had forgotten we were there for a purpose; I was busy swatting mosquitoes which the cigarettes we prudently cupped in our palms failed to drive away. Shouting and gunfire almost above my head broke into that silence as if all hell had been let loose. Because of its intensity, that moment when those glaring smudges of uniforms dashed shrieking toward us seemed interminable, but it had all happened so swiftly that, before I could think, my hands had gone up and the nozzle of an automatic was digging into my chest. In that position, I caught sight of Deptuła. He came out from behind the trees slowly and, sucking on his pipe, stood gloating over his work.

The memory of his small black eyes tormented me for years after the war with the desire for revenge. Although as a Mazurian he probably never left that region, I stifled the temptation to take a trip up there and give myself at least the satisfaction of letting him feel my power over him.

But vengeance was in the air everywhere then, and nothing came of it but universal despair and bitterness. In the autumn of 1945, the few days I spent in a certain village near Danzig left me with feelings of loathing and sadness. Germans were being evacuated from the area then. Some woman named Müller, who had tried in vain to defend herself by pointing out that she had harbored allied prisoners, committed suicide there, together with her children, by jumping into the Vistula. More or less at the same time, my mother died of typhus in this village; she, in turn, had lost her Lithuanian homeland in the East.

We were herded along at a fast clip through the forest. One arm breaking from the cursed pharmacist's suitcase, the second, under cover of darkness, maneuvering in my inside pocket to tear up some incriminating pieces of paper. Pretending to cough, I stuffed them into my mouth. The taste of the print was repulsive. At the police station in Kleine Leschinen, they did not search us, and Sophia, lying down on the cell floor, which was spread with straw, declared that as long as the Gestapo had not been called in, all was not lost.

Here the commandant enters. The terrible bellowing that came from the throat of that fat Bavarian might have been cause for alarm, but at the same time something playful lurked in the creases around his eyes. He did not remain indifferent to the stream of conversation that poured from Sophia, who, suddenly transformed into a *grande dame*, related a moving tale that was totally false. Doubtless the exceptionally favorable circumstances of life in this corner, certainly one of the quietest of wartime Europe, had taken the edge off his disposition. Next morning he told us he had telephoned to the Gestapo in Ortelsburg and that we were to be handed over. But his subordinate, after taking us in a horse-drawn buggy to Willenberg, needed no encouragement to accept my invitation to stop at a bar; after half a bottle of cognac he started showing me photos of his family and giving me to understand that the time had come to take ourselves off. We crawled under the barrier at the frontier. No one stopped us.

We moved along slowly from village to village, over sandy roads which the wheels on the peasant carts churned up quietly. Once we caught sight of a local concentration camp that stood on a plain. A column of prisoners was just returning from work. As they passed through the gates, their singing, which contrasted sharply with their gray, extinguished faces, cut me to the quick. Guards armed with rifles and whips completed the procession. We were shown the greatest friendliness, free from any trace of fear, in villages inhabited by descendants of the petty gentry. They simply did not acknowledge a foreign occupation. Compared to peasant villages, theirs had more carefully constructed buildings and all the residents bore the same name – that of their common ancestor. To avoid confusion, everyone tacked a nickname onto his surname.

In the little town of Ostrołęka my fatal curiosity once again drew me out on a little walk, away from the house where a fat woman, who quartered meat for the black market, had treated us to hospitality. My need to store up details of the human landscape in my own memory was invincible. Wooden fences plastered with German notices plunged me into a reverie on the metamorphoses of reality; that dream consisted mostly in amazement at the infinite number of changes that one man may see in the course of his own lifetime. Suddenly roused by the sound of a human voice, I saw in front of me a leather-coated officer of the Gestapo. Something barked and hit me in the face. My cap fell, I bent over to retrieve it, and when I had straightened up, the echo of his curses was still hanging in the air while his back disappeared into the distance. I did not understand. I lacked the following information: on seeing a German, all local people were obliged to step aside and take off their caps. 'Ach, you are lucky!' said our hostess when I told her about my accident. 'You are lucky he did not check your papers!'

The territory annexed to the German Reich ended just beyond the little town. Never in my life had I crossed a 'green border' like this one, although I had seen a good many since my childhood. The theory went that the best time to cross was at noon, because all the guards ate lunch then; the theory was known to everyone, including the guards. Through a forest of pines heated by the sun, groups of men and women, bent over by the load of their sacks and bundles, advanced in extended battle order, crouching behind trees, crawling along the moss, then making a run for it to the accompaniment of shots from all sides. These men and women were peasant smugglers carrying food products to be sold in Warsaw. Although I had changed into a wild rabbit and was painfully out of breath, I appreciated that spectacle of a moving forest where there was safety in numbers, as thoroughly as if I had been sitting in a movie theater. That whole horde then crammed onto the train, hens cackled from baskets, geese honked, piglets squealed under the benches, people talked about prices and policemen, the coach smelled of cheap tobacco. We were in the Government-General.

Some may find this description of one journey too detached, as if the physical discomfort of a whole night spent wading in water on the peat bog did not personally concern me, or as if my cheeks after being struck by the Gestapo officer did not burn. I doubt, however, that my detachment is due to the passage of time, which mitigates all painful experiences. Intense feelings or a groan torn from me by the strain did not ruffle a deep-seated indifference, a self-forgetfulness that could perhaps better be described as the sensitivity of a camera, ready to register everything that is visible. As I crawled on all fours over the pine needles, I enlarged in my disinterested imagination a drawing of a twig or an ant carrying its load, and shots rang out against the background, for example, of a line from Paul Valéry: '*Ce toit tanquille où marchent les colombes.*'

The world was imperturbable, magnificent. I loved it because with every turn it offered itself to me ever new, ever different, and I sailed with it as once I had with the Rhine River, meeting the unexpected at every bend. Both what I had read and what I myself had written about the Great Finale paled now, and after a long quarantine I felt that I knew how to live for the day and for the hour. An unsuspected shape of existence could almost be discerned: an existence from which the superfluous, including the future, was removed, and yet, for all that, was no worse. And this descent, if we apply the measuring rod of social prestige, to the level of black slaves in colonial countries had put the highest form of liberty within my reach.

The G.G.

For a study of human madness, the history of the Vistula basin during the time it bore the curious name of 'Government-General' makes excellent material. Yet the enormity of the crimes committed here paralyzes the imagination, and this, no doubt, is why the massacres in the small Czech town of Lidice and in the small French town of Oradour are given more notice in the annals of Nazi-dominated Europe than the region where there were hundreds of Lidices and Oradours. With the hanging of Governor Frank by a verdict of the Nuremberg Court, one chapter of total war appeared to have come to a close. Its cruelties are not interesting. But the system introduced into the Government-General had nothing to do with the necessities of war; in fact, and this was obvious to every spectator of the events, it ran counter to the interests of the German Army. The colossal energies that were mobilized to implement this system – that is, wasted on purely arbitrary goals – ought to fill us with awe at a century in which ideology prevails over material advantage.

The colored peoples did not suspect, when they were subjugated by the white man, that they were already avenged at the moment of their fall. Their conquerors returned home with their greed and converted it into an idea of supremacy over inferior races – even white races. That idea acquired a life of its own and was found not only among advocates of naked force but also, in a veiled form, among many democrats.

In the experimental laboratory known as the Government-General, the Nazis divided the local population into two categories: Jews and Poles. The former were scheduled for complete extermination in the initial phase; the latter, in the next phase, were to be partially exterminated and partially utilized as a slave-labor force. The objective for the 'non-Aryan' category was nearly one hundred per cent realized, as is borne out by the approximate figure of three million slain. The plan for the 'Aryans' was fulfilled more slowly, and their number only decreased by about twelve per cent.

At the same time an economic revolution was set in motion, and it had durable effects: all of the large industrial plants and most of the large landed estates were confiscated and turned over to German administrators. After that the Communist revolution was easy – all the state had to do later on, when the Germans fled, was to take over those enterprises that now belonged to no one. There were even more important changes that affected both the white-collar and blue-collar segments of the urban population. It became increasingly difficult to earn money because the Polish administrative apparatus no longer existed, having been replaced by one that employed only the colonizers; and it was no better in industry, where wages were a mere formality. They were so out of line with prices that a week's salary bought food for only one day.

As a result, masses of people were driven into illegal activities, economic as well as political. There were certainly moral reasons why the Resistance movement in Poland developed on a larger scale than any other in Europe, but the disemployment of the intelligentsia, who had previously staffed commercial offices, universities, schools, radio, and the press, was equally significant. Not only office jobs were eliminated, but the entire school system was liquidated – with the exception of the elementary grades (a race of slaves has no need for learning); and the publishing of books and magazines was prohibited. In a short time, however, the Poles erected an underground state

– with underground financing, administration, school system, army, and press. The occupier's struggle against this mass movement was reminiscent of the adventures that white rulers had had on other continents, and it cost the Reich many losses in manpower and war matériel. Thus in Berlin it became common usage to read the abbreviation 'G.G.' as *Gangster Gau*; the adversary always has to be a gangster and a thief.

Two conclusions can be drawn from this system. One is that nineteenth-century science fostered a completely naive picture of history by creating contempt in the popular mind (nourished on brochures) for more complicated factors than mechanistic, material ones – in a sense, Hitler took Darwinism, 'the struggle for existence' and the 'survival of the fittest,' too seriously, and by identifying history with nature he ignored the limits of blind force. That naive outlook was overcome in Marx's analyses, and all the errors of his successors may be due to their neglect of his intention. Although the Nazis borrowed several ideas from the East, such as propaganda, political police, and concentration camps (it is not hard to imagine where the sign *'Arbeit macht frei'* on the gate at Auschwitz came from), they saw the secret of power only in monstrous crimes because they were too inferior intellectually to go beyond vulgarized biology. The loathing these men showed for intellectuals was a defensive reflex against a real threat; they guessed the danger lurking in any analysis of effective political action.

The second conclusion is unflattering to the professors who, busy with their facts and figures, treat them as valuable in themselves regardless of their interpretation, or, worse, who serve them in a nationalistic sauce. Generations of German professors had studied the Slavic world, but all their graphs and statistics were useless. From the point of view of German interests, Nazi policy, after the take-over of Poland, the Ukraine, and Byelorussia, was nonsense.

The four years I spent in Warsaw were no exception to the general rule, and every new day was a gift that defied probability. When I arrived, walls were being built around one-third of the city, into which the Jewish population was being herded. The gates to the ghetto were not closed yet, and we could still visit our friends. To discourage 'Aryans' from such visits, signs were hung on the gate: 'Jews, Lice, Typhus.' But if those who were locked behind the walls had only extinction to look forward to – either from hunger, or from a bullet, or later from something vague that soon acquired the more concrete form of gas chambers – those outside the walls, who were swept away in the street round-ups that populated Auschwitz, and who had lost all prospects of earning an honest living, also knew they were running a race against time. Life, as for primitive man, once more depended on the seasons of the year. Autumn was the hardest because potatoes and coal had to be gotten for the long, hopeless winter. With spring, dreams of Germany's imminent defeat would make their appearance.

During those four years, I, and many like me, unlearned Western civilization, if what it teaches can be boiled down, more or less, to respect for money and the feeling that one has some kind of rights. Practically everyone I knew found himself in the financial situation of artistic bohemians, and all of us had the role of criminals hunted by the police. There were no grounds for being certain that one would eat next week, but this was accepted serenely. My friend, the novelist George Andrzejewski, invented a 'theory of the last penny' which I can recommend to everyone as tried and tested. It propounds the following: at the very moment when you have nothing in your pocket but your last penny, something *has* to happen. And it always did.

The steps I took to encourage destiny a bit give some idea of the possibilities that were open to us then. I began by trading such things as Players and Woodbine cigarettes and whiskey (war booty from Dunkirk; it circulated on the black market), as well as less elegant articles like blood sausage and ladies' underwear. Today this sounds amusing, but my despair, if I returned home without a sale was genuine.

Shortly afterward, I began to sell a completely different sort of product: my new volume of poetry, printed on a ditto machine and laboriously sewn together by Janka, my future wife. As far as I know, it was the first literary work published in occupied Warsaw. More or less at the same time, on George's initiative, a typewritten literary journal was put together, and we filled it with anti-Nazi articles.

One day I heard that workers were needed to dig out the remains of the French Institute's bombed library. The rescue effort was sponsored by the University Library. Like all libraries in Poland, it had been closed to the public and subordinated to a German central office, but its personnel had been kept on. Despite the salaries, which were below starvation level, the Polish employees loyally stayed on – besides, librarians are a special tribe; they are capable of feeding themselves on their very love for books. Having been assigned to a team of workers who loaded and transported the packing cases, I saw my opportunity and clung to the library for good. Now I could take home piles of books in various languages and immerse myself in reading. I owed my chance to become a porter to the new director of libraries, a tiny German Slavicist who had decided to protect himself at all costs from going to the front until the end of the war. With this in mind he and his adviser, a Pole by the name of Pulikowski, had elaborated a gigantic plan, requiring at least ten years to accomplish, that made both of them indispensable. With unshakable logic, the plan envisaged the rearrangement of the book collections from Warsaw's three largest libraries and the transport of millions of volumes by horsedrawn cart so that one library would contain Polish works only: the second, foreign works only; and the third, works on music, theater, and art. It was an undertaking to match moving the Alps, and in its *systematisch* approach faithfully duplicated the whole Government-General – except that its madness was bloodless.

The Polish personnel regarded the small docent with disdainful indifference, reserving the whole of their hatred for his adviser. This man must have experienced great inner turmoil. Raised in Germany, married to a German woman, speaking only German at home, he believed, it seems, that the New Order was permanent. My colleagues, porters and clerks, in the library warned each other of the traitor's approach by clearing their throats. Many a time, as we sat back on our heels to rest or crouched in an alcove to smoke a cigarette, he would try to sneak up on us, treading softly in his rubber-soled shoes. His overseer's zeal, however, did not protect him from death in 1944. Who killed him – whether Germans or Poles – I no longer remember.

Physical labor, interspersed with moments of reading, agreed with me, and I prospered on potato and carrot soups. I was grateful to the war for one thing: the end of my bureaucratic career. In the dark recesses of the stacks no police could have ferreted out the underground publications stuffed between the volumes, and that was convenient. Riding through the city with a load of books, I warmed myself in the sun, stretching out on the packing cases; I felt as if I were melting into a fascinating city-jungle with its waves of panic and intermittent bursts of gunfire. In winter we sometimes made a detour to one of the employee's houses, where we warmed up with a shot of pure alcohol. I grew attached to our whole collective there at the library, with its Polish head, the historian Dr. Lewak. Of course the trifling pennies we received as salaries were not enough, and beyond the initial period, when I looked for the moral support that comes from belonging to a group, I showed up only now and then for work in order not to lose the right to keep myself supplied with books.

The underground state grew in strength little by little, and, like all writers, I began to receive small grants from clandestine funds. The source of such funds was the high exchange rate of the dollar on the black market. Dollars came through secret channels from England or were parachuted from planes, and you could tell whether or not there had been a recent drop from the way the black-market rates fluctuated. The literary commissions increased, too. I worked with a clandestine unit whose name should come as a surprise, considering that such people are usually thought of as undisciplined: an actors' unit. Theater in Poland, however, has never been a purely capitalistic enterprise; in any case, its members have always seen themselves as high priests of art – and that imposes duties. This clandestine group prescribed a code of behavior for an actor toward the occupier and forbade acting in Nazi-licensed spectacles. It won high respect in Warsaw from the time when a certain actor, who had begun to collaborate, was shot in his own apartment. The group was headed by the distinguished director Edmund Wierciński, who with the help of his fellow-actors was preparing a radical reform of the theater for after the war. They were debating the repertoire and ordering translations of plays or original works. This activity served my literary workshop well. The actors themselves worked hard, and to this day their excellent clandestine performances in private homes or monasteries are still fresh in my memory. Edmund's wife, Maria, who was also a director, set a record of her own as a propagator of subversive poetry: she organized over one hundred and fifty clandestine poetry readings.

The breakthrough which the year 1939 had been forced me to revise my habits. Time was precious; not to use it as I should, to drift as I had before the war, would have meant shirking my most important duty. After all, I had run from Stalin's state to be able to think things over for myself instead of succumbing to a world view imposed from without. There was complete freedom here, precisely because National Socialism was an intellectual zero. However, I had to solve the problem of hope, or, rather, to find a position from which hope and despair were equally irrelevant. My chances of survival and of seeing with my own eyes what came out of this caldron were negligible. With some effort, I finally obeyed Martin Luther's advice: when asked what he would do if he knew tomorrow was going to be the end of the world, he said, 'I would plant apple trees.'

The library books convinced me that my Polish, French, and Russian were insufficient. I had had enough of French harping on Arthur Rimbaud and Stéphane Mallarmé. So I resolved to discover Anglo-Saxon poetry and began to learn English. After I could read with a dictionary, further progress went swiftly. (In German I understood, and to this day understand, almost nothing except *Hände hoch!* and *Alle Männer 'rrraus!* Not much, for the language of Goethe.)

Since I, like everyone else, was tortured by the why of Europe's fall, I tried to clarify my thought by writing about certain philosophical aspects of literature. I intended those essays – on Daniel Defoe, Balzac, Stendhal, André Gide, Tolstoy, William James, and two Polish authors (Stanisław Ignacy Witkiewicz and Marian Zdziechowski) – as a book. A few were published; others, such as an attack on André Gide, I preferred to leave in manuscript because of their obsessive nature. In those days, however, they filled more than a private need, since they were read at clandestine gatherings where they provoked serious discussion. Despite the lack of any legal publications (Poles were forbidden to publish even translations from the German), intellectual activity flourished; there was development; and by the end of the war many of us could compare the distance we had come from our old selves to the passage of a whole geological era.

The anthology of poetry I put together had a more immediate function. It contained poems, then circulating in handwritten copies, from the pen of local or émigré poets. Called *The Independent Song*, it appeared in 1942 in a nicely printed little edition; the publisher considered it the success of the underground market. That same year, I was pleased to be able in a small way to defend France's good name, which Nazi propagandists had dragged in the dirt. The whole affair proves how difficult it is for totalitarian systems to combat the word, which slips over borders more rapidly and more effectively than people on the outside imagine. While publishing *A travers le désastre* in Canada, Jacques Maritain did not suspect that his work, which was aimed at the Vichy government, would reach distant Poland. A certain Dutch merchant brought it to Warsaw. In my translation and with my very pro-French introduction, the text was set in extra-small type and printed in a vest-pocket format. My further penetration into English poetry also turned to my advantage: commissioned by the actors' organization, I pored over Shakespeare's *As You Like It* for several months, preparing a new translation since, in Edmund's opinion, the existing translations did not lend themselves well to stage delivery. Bucolic Shakespeare proved to be first-rate therapy. On Edmund's suggestion, backed by a fee, I also wrote a *Prologue* for the reopening of the Warsaw theaters after the war. What happened to the manuscript, whether any copies were rescued from the fire in the city, I have no idea. The tone of the *Prologue* (a dialogue between a humanist and a politician) was, I think, somewhat too elevated, since the relentless march of events was to bring defeat to the humanists.

The proliferation of the underground press irritated both George and myself. The death of many printers, editors, and carriers went unredeemed by the scant value of these miniature weeklies and dailies. Communiqués about Allied victories were scattered among articles that led the public astray with their false optimism. For this reason we were in favor of publishing books. They afforded space for analysis and were easier to distribute. Usually a book received an innocent-looking cover with a title like *A Handbook for Grain Cultivation*, and it was always antedated. But in our attempts to secure funds we rarely succeeded, for censorship functioned in the underground, making sure that all toed the London-government line, which did not look kindly upon speculation about the future; that is, upon any sort of ideological 'tommyrot' from intellectuals. Yet, if only for ourselves, we wanted to gain a clear perspective, and to do that we chose the form of letters. Every time we met (George and I lived at opposite ends of town) we exchanged our philosophical epistles. A whole volume thus unfolded, a document of immediate reactions to historical reality.

Although these activities kept me busy, they were marginal. What really interested me was poetry, or, to be more exact, the extremely difficult task of discovering its new and vital patterns. From the stress of daily tragedy for millions of human beings, the word had burst and fallen to pieces. All previous forms had become meaningless. The emotional gibberish so widespread then made me feel ashamed, of myself, too, whenever I wrote something that might flatter those who were waiting for just such outpourings. This is why I dislike a couple of my poems that became popular in occupied Warsaw. No more than three years later I dug through to deeper layers, greatly aided by my meditations on English poetry. This did not mean imitating, for the disparity in experience was too great: T. S. Eliot's *The Waste Land*, for example, made somewhat weird reading as the glow from the burning ghetto illuminated the city skyline.

So I spent my time among books and papers from which my earnings came. There was also 'The Firm,' an institution a bit too colorful to pass up here, mainly because of its founder. When we studied law together in Wilno, W. was mistakenly evaluated by all of us. He was a tall, anemic youth who spoke very little, as if every sentence cost too much physical effort. The son of a miner from Silesia, he had a definite Leftist bent, but at the same time was extremely pious. I roomed with him for a while in the student dormitory. And from then on I always remembered him as a man kneeling at his bedside, hands folded, engrossed in either morning or evening prayers. True, even then I was puzzled by his mysterious ability to combine contemplation and action. He took an energetic part in politics at the university; and when he stepped onto the platform, this quiet boy suddenly became a leader, capable of polemics and violent invective; then, instead of his usual half-whisper, he barked in a hard, metallic voice. Valued as an organizer and a strategist, he performed various functions in the Leftist-liberal bloc. No one, however, could have foreseen his later metamorphosis into a trader worthy of the Wild West.

He founded The Firm in Wilno during the fall of 1941, while the German Army trudged toward the Volga. In a few months his profits soared from nothing to millions, and soon The Firm had two branches: one in Minsk, the capital of Byelorussia, and the other in Warsaw. Granted proper Nazi authorization on the ground of being 'useful for the Army,' the outfit was supplied with all sorts of passes and permits and allegedly traded in goods. In fact it dealt in the black-market purchase and sale of currency. The greater part, if not all, of the truck shipments consisted of

weapons for partisan detachments. In this W.'s talent
for high diplomacy nearly reached the level of genius,
because his trucks moved unharassed through the
forests of Byelorussia, which were controlled by
Partisans of varying colors. As a financial power
The Firm secured privileges for itself from the Germans
through bribery, paying out a regular bonus to a few
dignitaries; it also maintained its own workshop for
making false documents, and ran an effective rescue
operation for those threatened with arrest – especially
Jews, many of whom owe their lives to it. The Firm
often transported them, carefully packaged, from city
to city. Was W. a merchant-conqueror, a politician, or
an apostle of love of one's neighbor? It would be
impossible to separate these three qualities of his.

The Firm's headquarters in Warsaw, where the
major activity had shifted as the front moved gradually
westward, did not look much like a commercial
enterprise. In a large room, amid the disorder of tires,
crates, engine parts, and drums of gasoline, truck
drivers slouched with their feet up on sofas, chatting
lazily in a Wilno dialect and smoking cigarettes. This
brigade, composed of 'my boys' from Wilno suburbs,
knew the complex organization inside and out. It was
a team of completely trustworthy men who were
treated by their boss as equals. In the second room
W.'s partner, K., hung on the telephone. He was a fat

Latvian Jew with a black mustache, armed with Aryan birth certificates to the tenth generation.

W. made a lot of money, which he invested as if he were playing a lottery; and he was right in judging all objects and values as fly-by-night, since the apartment houses in Warsaw, for example, were soon burned down, and the lots they stood on nationalized. He did choose to put money into manuscripts of books, since he intended to found a publishing house after the war. Not only did he buy a couple of my manuscripts, but he named me his agent. We made up contracts carefully, although I could never quite suppress the feeling that I was participating in some sort of make-believe and that sums of money passed from hand to hand simply to circulate.

As agent, I endeavored to bring about a merger between two nonexistent publishing houses, both of which relied on the black market for income. Negotiations were protracted, as they usually are when what is at stake is a treasure on a nonexistent island. The high point of my effort was a dinner, to which both parties had been invited, at one of the more elegant restaurants run by unemployed actors and painters who knew how to create settings of charm and grace. We drank the best French wines and cognacs, were entertained by a singer who played the accordion, but instead of sealing the agreement, that feast turned out to be the preface to further, hopeless quarrels over the percentage of shares. Yet all three of us knew that underneath those financial wrestlings was laughter. W., his would-be partner, and I belonged to the same Socialist organization – an offshoot of the group in Wilno which operated at the beginning of the war. When I took the oath (I swore to be 'loyal to the people' or something of that sort), it was also to the sound of bottles being uncorked and in a similarly arty restaurant; I remember that two of Poland's best young composers, Lutosławski and Panufnik, furnished the entertainment, playing on two pianos.

To live with one's cowardice is bitter. Unfortunately, I did not know how to get rid of it. Perhaps in other Nazi-dominated countries the very act of publishing anti-Nazi works was cause enough for pride, but not in Poland. Here the whole collectivity made demands and exerted pressure. Yet the danger was no greater than walking down the street. When everything is outside the law, nothing is outside it, and prohibitions have no meaning. One Sunday afternoon I saw a family: a man and a woman pushing a baby buggy; the Gestapo car rolled up to them slowly. The man, seeing a revolver nozzle aimed at him, put up his hands; they thrust him into the car and moved off to further hunting – for sport. To play Providence, to be able to point your finger at someone and say, 'That's the one,' is no small treat for human vanity. People caught in this way filled the delivery quotas for the death camps at Auschwitz and Maidanek; their names could also be read on the lists of those shot or hung at 'hostages'' executions.

There would be no point today in trying to convince myself or others that I had any sort of talent for heroism. I admit it openly: I turned cold with fear even at home if I happened to meet our apartment manager's eyes with their veiled threat, knowing that he suspected one of our guests was a Jew. (The 'people'? The 'people' cared, above all, about saving their own skin.) The manager once drove away two Jewish children who used to eat dinner at our house, and they were afraid to come any more. They slept somewhere in unfinished houses or in ruins; I spotted them once; the older boy, a ten-year-old, was sitting on a pile of bricks, reading a newspaper to the younger. But out of shame I did not go up to them; I did not have a penny on me and had nothing to give them. Such homeless children, runaways from the ghetto, were shot down in the street by people in green uniforms who left the corpses for the municipal authorities to bury.

A desire to regain their dignity drove practically all young people into the service of the underground army, known as the Home Army (A.K.), whose hierarchy was controlled by the London émigré government. Many of its divisions operated in the forests; others specialized in assassination attempts on high German officials who were responsible for crimes against the Poles. Because of the extreme difficulty of such counterterroristic acts, the conspirators, like the Japanese suicide pilots, had to give full consent to their own death. The Home Army built up an extensive network, and among the feats of its intelligence section working for the Allied cause, not the least was the discovery of the first German experiments with the V-2's. For most young people in Warsaw, membership in the A.K. meant obedience to the orders of one's immediate superior, classes in military theory, or, if possible, practical training in the art of warfare.

Even though the actors' group was connected in various ways with the army, I did not join the A.K.; nor were my literary colleagues, on the whole, eager to rush into the fray, gun in hand. By the age of thirty, one has already acquired a certain number of habits, not necessarily good ones. The individual invariably argues: 'I don't want to die,' which can be translated as 'I have more important tasks ahead of me.' In other words, if the individual says this, he shows that he lacks the humility necessary for cooperating with others. I realized in the first phase of the war that a resolve that breaks through our smallness is born only out of a powerful emotional impulse, which in turn is inseparably bound up with a belief in the purpose of our sacrifice.

These reflections may seem cynical and brutal. Yet, I never even asked myself if it was my duty to plunge deeper into conspiracy. Not only did I now lack the impulse, but I was restrained by my passionate hostility to the leaders of the Home Army. The political fantasy of prewar Warsaw – with its slogan 'We will not yield an inch,' with its conviction that if the Germans struck, the Polish Army would occupy Berlin in a matter of days – was only amplified by the defeat, and the whole conspiratorial apparatus fed on an illusion, pumping into itself a gloomy national ecstasy. There had to be a bright tomorrow, but whoever dared to hint that it depended upon the choice of political systems and on the international power game exposed himself to dangers that were not always platonic.

Beneath the smooth surface of common hatred for the occupier, a struggle was going on for control of the future. In other words, prospective posts were assigned not according to merit but to political acceptability. As a result, despite the existence of a Council of Parties that included Socialists and Populists, there was a tendency on the part of the military brass to return to the prewar Rightist pattern. The country, as before the war, was to be a 'rampart' in the East, backed by its Western Allies; no one could suspect otherwise. But since events continually gave the lie to this hope, the air was poisoned by the fumes of self-delusive and illogical thinking. My individualism may not have been a virtue, but at least it protected me from succumbing to collective moods and impelled me to turn away from what I considered spasms of the dying past. For that matter, writers, unable to find their way out of the snare, were the first to rebel against this exalted self-befuddlement. Beginning in 1943, some of their works showed a clearly satirical cast.

We always meet those whom we are ready to meet. The city offered him to me no sooner than my need made his appearance necessary. We had known each other fleetingly before the war, because of his tie with philosophical circles in Warsaw. The University's philosophy seminar often met at the home of my close friend Bolesław Miciński, the philosopher-poet. I once went to a lecture my future teacher gave on phenomenology after his return from Prague, where he had completed his studies at Charles University. But now I saw him differently. His closest friends called him Tiger because of his rapacity in argument, which reduced others to the status of grass-eating animals. A master of flexibility, of innocent ambush, of apparent absentmindedness, he fell upon his victim in one leap, and annihilated him with his irony, usually expressed in the form of parody and pantomime. Had it not been for him, my strenuous efforts to resist a lyricism of self-pity (as well as to reject the political stance imposed by my environment) might have come to nothing. As a catalyzer, he was indispensable.

Juliusz Tadeusz K. and his wife, Irena, rarely left their house; by Nazi racial laws, he was a *Mischling* and she deserved immediate removal from the face of the earth. They earned their livelihood making cigarettes. The tobacco on the black market came from peasants who cultivated it illegally. Fermented and cut in small processing plants, it could then be rolled in cigarette paper or in tubes. With practice, one could work up an almost machine-like production speed; finished cigarettes were put in boxes of a hundred. In addition, Tiger edited a journal for one of the numerous underground organizations (to make it more amusing, it was an organization of non-commissioned officers) and wrote political articles. Both of them sought peace and wisdom in Plato, whom they read in Greek.

It is difficult to achieve a distance from events, living in a mechanical slaughterhouse whose conveyor belt unceasingly carries off bodies of butchered human beings. In such circumstances, the future is annihilated and one compensates for its loss by creating an illusory tomorrow where truth and justice will triumph. This is precisely why almost all the inhabitants of Warsaw could not step past the threshold that victory over the Germans stood for: a promise of paradise. That the war was only an episode they might have understood, but to understand this and to know it with one's whole being are two different things. Tiger never dissociated the war from what preceded it or from what was to follow. What prompted him was not philosophical indifference but philosophical hatred.

Hatred for people who live badly. Hatred not only for the Nazis – even less for the Nazis, because they were condemned in advance to a dreadful punishment – but also for most of their adversaries, the Polish patriots. During great catastrophes one should try to live well; that, for him, was the only guarantee of salvation. What does that mean? It means not sinning in thought against the structure of the universe, which is meaningful. One sins by falling into hallucinations, by absolutizing impermanent values, by despising our mind, which leads us toward a mathematical ordering of cause and effect. Tiger had suffered many humiliations from those who rallied round the Fatherland and who were enemies of everything that appeared to threaten it. Did their heroic struggle against Hitler change them? Not in the least. They shared the same cult of action and the same contempt for the intellect. Taking them as an example, Tiger built up his own theology of history as of a being that occasionally shows a foot or a finger – and woe to those who disregard the sign! Poland's underground was self-sacrificing as perhaps no other in Europe. But for just that reason, Tiger watched it with horror and pity, realizing the full extent of the tragedy. Call it dialectical skill, or political imagination, or a sense of historical humor, he foresaw, as if in a crystal ball, that a sad future lay in store for the conspirators. The mocking impersonations he did of his superiors in the underground organization of officers and noncoms used to undo me; the more skillfully he played a part in front of them, the better he penetrated them. True, some hunch put them on their guard against that demon of intelligence: at first they agreed to publish his book on democracy, written under the pseudonym of Michael Psellos (he liked the works of English historians on Byzantium), but on second thought they withdrew their offer. Tiger also predicted what would become of the émigré government after the war: in England two rival newspapers would combat each other, the *London Bee* and the *Scottish Hornet*; 'and they will spend the rest of their days that way.' Externally, he was careful to keep up faultless appearances. Whenever he met the priest who lived next door, he always bowed and greeted him vigorously: 'My respects, Father!' He used to say that paying homage to an ecclesiastical person created an excellent political image.

A democrat of the Left, he kept a tactical distance from the Communists. The latter, as agents of a foreign power, were avoided in Warsaw like lepers. Contrary to other countries of Europe, in Poland the Communists not only did not set the tone of the Resistance movement but, due to their stigma, could only scramble about on the sidelines. One sometimes had the opportunity to talk with a couple of them in literary circles, but they were in an unenviable position and used poor arguments. When asked about the year 1939, the deportations, and the concentration camps, they shrugged their shoulders: 'What's a million people more or a million less in the light of historical evolution? A trifle.' Tiger, however, forbade me to speak badly of Russia because in doing so one might offend the Ear. According to him, a gigantic, majestic Ear – History, Providence, or Fate – they blended together in his thinking – bent over the world. Tiger must have been born a Hegelian. It was normal for him to speak in metaphors, and here he meant that we should not harbor enmity toward Russia, for in so doing we lose our ability to judge soberly and to face up to future events. Open conflict broke out between us. I reproached him with an evasion of knowledge, for he did not even know Russian. I wanted him to step into the future with open eyes, but he, of course, had already put an equal sign between the words 'real' and 'good,' and this made me angry.

Wisdom, yes, but shameful, because in thus conversing with each other we could not warn anyone, and the Home Army (like Mihajłović's army, except that Poland had no Tito) advanced toward its unhappy fate. By 'warn' I do not mean the foretelling of a Communist victory. No one then saw clearly what was to come. The whole thing was unfolding on much deeper levels than the slick surfaces of newspaper articles, and it was because of this that the barriers between people were insurmountable. Some attitudes are foredoomed, so detached are they from reality. Thus, instead of arguing, all Tiger had to do when assailed by their musty odors was simply to imitate a pure maiden who embroiders her flag and sings a patriotic song about Polish uhlans. One cannot live by crippling one's awareness, by doing violence to oneself in order to remain on a level that has become intolerable. That epoch required, at the very least, a new sense of touch. This has nothing to do with afterthoughts; that is, with the question of whether the country could have avoided later misfortunes. By touch, I perceived a wall. And I realized, having profited from Tiger's cautionary whispers, that we do not necessarily have to bloody our fists on that wall or to bow down before it in humility. But no politician could have seen this, and the Socialists who were too intelligent to believe in their own manifestos bored me. Right or wrong, I considered my poetry a kind of higher politics, an unpolitical politics.

Pity, sympathy, and anger gave that poetry directness. Despite the circumstances, and despite the images of ruins and destruction taken from my surroundings, it was a triumphal poetry. It celebrated the holiday of my coming into health, for the first time in my life. A recovery from that powerlessness when everything, both in the world and in us, is so obscure and tied up in knots that we lack the courage to be sharp, like a diamond cutting glass. I had written poems on 'social' themes and had been bothered by their artificiality. I had practiced 'pure' poetry and had been no less irritated. Only now had the contradiction vanished. Now even the most personal poem translated a human situation and contained a streak of irony that made it objective. Something had gone on inside me after I admitted a brutal truth to myself: Poland's prewar society, which had shackled me with its subtle collective censorship, meant absolutely nothing to me, and I was indifferent to its latest pathetic and messianic embodiment. Virtue had gagged me up to then; one had to throw it off and proclaim that what appeared to be the end was not the end of either tradition or literature or art. I knew I had wasted years thrashing about blindly in some kind of quagmire. But finally I had worked myself out of it. To track down and root out of oneself all vestiges of the past – what disruption and what temptation to regret! But also what purity of air, what nakedness, what readiness to face the future!

My liberation had a political significance for which Tiger was responsible: the country's sufferings and the 'national front' had screened my hatred for the Right, but now it burst forth openly. I differed sharply, however, from the Communists; they assuaged their grievances with doctrine, which put a wall between them and the concrete: hence the weakness of their writing. Doctrinally I was very far from them. An inner political liberation may be filtered through our being in various ways. The 'naive poems' I wrote then have a somewhat deceptive simplicity; they are really a metaphysical tract, an equivalent, in colors and shapes, of the school blackboard on the Rue d'Assas where Father Lallemant drew his Thomistic circles.

I also accepted my none-too-enviable place on earth and the dark instinct that led me to Warsaw. Had I emigrated then, I would probably have remained stuck in my prewar phase. Had I struck off for the East, my protest against inhumanity would have driven me back into undiscriminating Polish patriotism, and I would never have broken through my shell. Here, I had had a decisive experience. In 1943, I set down my future duties quite clearly: neither the 'pure poetry' of Abbé Bremond and its later theoreticians, nor Russian Socialist realism. This experience also anticipated my later reserve toward Western literature. By fusing individual and historical elements in my poetry, I had made an alloy that one seldom encounters in the West.

Little by little the time was drawing near for the destruction of Warsaw. The uprising was a blameworthy, lightheaded enterprise; it completely confirmed Tiger's diagnosis – although two hundred thousand corpses do carry weight, and no one can tell what shapes the legend may take, or what influence it may exert during the decades and centuries to come. Moreover, the last week of July, 1944, explains some of the reasons for it. Handfuls of people stood on street corners, watching with a quiet smile as trucks were loaded with wardrobes, mirrors, rugs – the contents of German offices and private homes. They were fleeing. No one was afraid of them anymore. The posters that had been tacked up, ordering all males to report for work on the fortifications, were received with jeers. You could already hear Russian artillery fire. Rumors of an armed uprising were greeted joyfully: a chance to throw oneself at one's tormentors and take revenge . . . Soon, however, came news that there would be no uprising. One of my Socialist colleagues told me that to take any sort of action now, when Mikołajczyk, the premier of the London government, was flying to Moscow, would be nonsense. Stalin was too clever to negotiate with anyone using such a trump card, and whoever tried to outsmart him would never be forgiven.

The military leaders (caught between two fires, because the Russian Radio broadcasts called for the taking up of arms) did not enter into such subtleties; as a result their judgment was incompetent. The command was given so suddenly that it found most of the units without weapons. Their intention was probably no different from that of the men who started the gun battle in Paris as the American Army was approaching. The outcome was entirely different.

That day, the first of August, Janka and I were walking over to Tiger's for an afterdinner chat and a cup of tea. I had something terribly important to discuss; namely, my new translation of an English poem. On leaving for a walk one should never be too sure of returning home, not only because something may happen to one personally, but also because the house may cease to exist. Our walk was to last a long time.

Ten carefree minutes under a cloudless sky. Then, unexpectedly, everything burst and my angle of vision changed as I found myself advancing on all fours. This outer-city district, where vegetable gardens and sparsely scattered houses bordered the fields, was so thickly planted with S.S. troops that the insurrectionists never managed to capture it. Machine guns fired at anything that moved. Not far away some friends lived; but when neither running nor walking is possible, three hundred feet is a whole journey. Heavy fire broke loose at our every leap, nailing us to the potato fields. In spite of this I never let go of my book – first of all out of respect for social ownership, since the book bore a call number of the University Library; secondly I needed it (although I could stop needing it). Its title: *The Collected Poems of T. S. Eliot*, in the Faber & Faber edition.

It was dawn of the next day by the time we crawled up to the island; that is, to a small modern flat with beautiful flowers in the courtyard; the open spaces around it made it seem completely cut off from the outside world. Yet during our two weeks of forced internment we did not run out of groats or potatoes or even coffee. From our host's bookcase I dug out a volume of sociological essays about prewar Poland, *The Young Generation of Peasants*, and plunged into a sorry reckoning with my own and my country's past, from time to time dropping flat on the floor as bullets traced long patterns across the plaster.

A kind of well in the cellar, which was connected to the fire hydrant, figured in one humiliating experience. The well was big enough for two to stand in comfortably, but there were eleven of us – all the men in the house. We hid in it when the rumble of huge S.S. tanks sounded in the vicinity. The women closed the metal cover over us, and inside we immediately began to suffocate. It was quite theatrical: in the light from the electric bulb I saw the mouths of fish thrown up on the sand and heads withering on stems of necks. A struggle also went on between those who preferred to suffocate and those who wanted to lift the cover. I suffocated, but with a nervous giggle. And anyway I did not know how real the danger was until one of us was picked up by the S.S. one day. He died running with upraised arms in front of a tank, along with a group of unlucky people like himself who were used as a human buffer in an attack on the insurrectionists' barricades.

Then the houses nearby caught fire and began to smoke. Since we were on the edge of the city, the only logical way out was across the fields. After much debate, our island crew divided up. Those who opted to remain behaved unreasonably. Our group, having made it over vegetable gardens, oat fields, and stubble, took shelter in an isolated building not far from the airport, a storehouse for grain. From the attic, we had a magnificent panorama of a white city on a plain over which billowed masses of black smoke pierced through with red tongues of flame. The noise of battle reached even to where we were: the rattle of machine guns, the laborious hammering of tank artillery, the flat sound of antiaircraft guns, bomb explosions. Since our neighborhood was the closest to us, I could make out our house, where my desk, the witness of so many inner struggles, stood. Under the artillery fire its façade wrinkled like a face rapidly growing old. It was probably then that all my worldly goods fell through to the floor below. At night, dots of varicolored lights moved over the city: they were Germans firing, and very effectively too, at Polish and British planes that were flying in to drop supplies; they were coming from Italy. We passed several days and nights in the granary, while the nearby highway was patrolled by so-called 'Vlasovians' (soldiers from auxiliary German Army divisions) recruited from various nationalities of the Soviet Union. To be more exact, they were taking advantage of their idleness to learn how to ride the bicycles they had captured. Of all things on earth, this, for some reason, seemed to me the most extravagant. They had chosen the slaughter of civilians as their vocation because, as their officers had told them in order to justify such a pleasure, Warsaw was a 'bourgeois city.' Those bodies of dead women we had passed in the fields were their work.

Among our group hiding in the warehouse there was one specimen who looked as if he had just emerged from the Tertiary, or at least the Victorian, era. A corpulent man with a short black mustache, he was wearing a black suit and a bowler. He raised his finger, sniffed, and said: 'Bad. It smells of a corpse in here.' And he was right. We could not prolong our rodent's life there, flattened out between sacks of grain. Opinions were again divided: some held that it was worse to go, others that it was worse to wait. Since we belonged to the latter, we set out as grass-hoppers were singing by the empty highway in the warmth of a sunny afternoon.

Is it possible to surround a city of over a million with a cordon of guards? We found out that it was when we were caught and put behind the barbed-wire fence of a camp. 'Camp' is saying too much: it was nothing more than the yard of some construction firm, with sleepy German soldiers guarding the gates. Every morning the daily catch was sent to a camp in the nearby small town of Pruszków. There people were sorted into transports, men and women separately, and sent off to concentration camps in Germany. At all costs we had to get out of there. I wrote secret notes to our companions in the granary, handing my appeal for help through the fence and trusting to the local children of that Warsaw suburb.

Human solidarity. Rescue showed up that evening in the form of a majestic nun. She commanded me severely to remember that I was her nephew. Her quiet, authoritative tone and the fluency of her German forced the soldiers into unwilling respect. Her conversation with the officer lasted an hour. Finally she appeared on the threshold: 'Hurry up, hurry up.' We passed through the main gate. I had never met her before and I never met her again. Nor did I ever know her name.

Happiness

Between the ages of seven and ten I lived in perfect happiness on the farm of my grandparents in Lithuania. The localities of our valley are mentioned for the first time around 1350 by the chronicles of the Teutonic Knights, who invaded the region while fighting my still-pagan ancestors. My grandparents' farm, where I was born, had belonged to my mother's family for several centuries, during which its landscape gradually changed, and I now know that I should be especially grateful to my great-grandfather, who, on a grassy slope descending to the river, planted many trees, creating a grovelike park. And he established orchards, two by the house, the third a little farther, beyond the old white-walled granary. It was long ago, and huge oaks and lindens made my fairyland, while orchards allowed me to discover the taste of apples and pears of many species.

I do not know the date when a new house replaced

the wooden one. Probably it was in the middle of the nineteenth century. The white walls hid not a brick structure but a wooden scaffolding covered with mortar. The inside was cool in summer and difficult to heat in winter by stoves that burned mostly birch logs. Many years later I found in Dutch paintings the images of interiors just like those in my childhood house.

I lived without yesterday or tomorrow, in the eternal present. This is, precisely, the definition of happiness. I ask myself whether I now mythologize that period of my life. We all build myths when speaking of the past, for a faithful reconstruction of fleeting moments is impossible. The question, however, remains: Why do some people speak of their childhoods as happy, others, as miserable? The extreme vividness and intensity of my experience forces me to believe in its authenticity. It was, I do not hesitate to say, an experience of enchantment with earth as a Paradise.

To tell about one's childhood usually is to tell about one's family, yet in this respect I must confess that for me adults resided in a hazy world, not my own. I was a lone child in a magic kingdom that I explored from early morning till dusk. My younger brother was then a baby, and I paid no attention to him, nor did I have any companions of my age. Thus I was a little Adam, running all day in a garden under trees that seemed to me even bigger than they were in reality, with my perceptions and fantasies unhampered by the sarcastic jeer of a demon.

What seems strange to me today is that at the age of seven I had already lived a story of adventures that could have provided memories for a whole lifetime. There were travels in military trains through Russia during World War I, when my father, a civil engineer, was drafted to build bridges for the czarist army; there was the Bolshevik revolution, with its perquisitions, escapes, fears, which I lived through in a town on the Volga. All that must have somehow persisted in me, yet it did not bring more awareness; on the contrary, it receded, perhaps thanks to self-protection's peculiar mechanism. I remained innocent, which means that I had not formed any judgment on the cruelty of the world.

Particular events that would have sufficed to impose such a judgment did not coagulate into any whole; rather, each one existed in my mind separately. Neither did the routine of life on a farm, with its unavoidable knowledge of the pain and death of animals, affect me much. When fishing, I concentrated on the goal of my action – to catch a fish – and did not reflect on the worm squirming at the hook's end, or on the pain of a little perch that, a hook placed in its body through an incision in its skin, served as bait for a pike. And

Czesław Miłosz

yet, who knows? Perhaps my future pessimism could be traced back to moments in my tender age, a pessimism reaching so far that as an adult I was to really value one philosopher only, the bitter Schopenhauer.

My happiness came, it seems, from, as William Blake would say, cleansing the gates of perception, in avidly seeing and hearing. A path in the shade of oaks led down to the river, and my river was never to abandon me throughout my life, wherever fate carried me, even during my years on the far shores of the Pacific. Its slow current allowed the growth of water lilies, and in certain places their pads covered the whole surface. Its banks, with their rim of calamus, were shaded by bushes and alder trees. I spent hours watching sunlight on water, movements of little water creatures and flights of dragonflies and . . . I am ready to call it daydreaming, yet it would not be correct, for this would suggest passivity, while my imagination was vividly active.

Thus as a child I was primarily a discoverer of the world, not as suffering but as beauty. The trees of the park, the orchards, and the river founded a separate realm of intensified, radiant reality more true than anything situated outside.

We often become aware of the harshness of the world through struggle with others, frequently with other children. On the farm I had nobody to compete with, nobody who would try to submit me to his or her will. Of course I often cried, for instance, when my mother would force me to abandon my playing and sit down to the impossible task of learning how to write the letters of the alphabet. Yet it was not a real pressure – this ordinarily comes from our peers, as I later had the occasion to convince myself, when I went to school in town.

Happiness experienced in childhood does not pass without a trace: the memory of ecstasy dwells in our body and possesses a strong curative power. As a young man I was somber and tormented; I showed a considerable talent for gathering wounds and bruises. Perhaps this was simply my line of fate, yet time and place might have had something to do with my depressive predisposition. In the thirties the Central European–Baltic area carried in its air premonitions of the crimes to be perpetrated. To the east, in Soviet Russia, millions of 'class enemies' were toiling and dying in the so-called corrective labor camps. I was twenty-two when neighboring Germany voted Hitler into the position of absolute ruler. A few years later the mass murder committed at his orders horrified humanity.

My religion and philosophy were marked by a dark vision, and I was inclined to believe that the universe was created as a result of a cosmic catastrophe, perhaps by Satan himself. Brought up a Roman Catholic, I felt the attraction of the old Manichaean heresy. It suited the time when, to use the expression of Emmanuel Lévinas, 'God left in 1941.' The poetry I wrote before the war and later in Nazi-occupied Poland would have been utterly without hope if not for my awareness of the beauty of the things of this earth, and that beauty was incomprehensible, as it coexisted with horror.

Many years later, at the age of eighty, I returned to the place of my birth and childhood. The landscape had changed, and probably those changes were more radical than any made there by man since the Middle Ages. Lithuania, an independent country before World War II, was occupied in 1940 by the Soviet Union, and the collectivization of agriculture was enforced by the Communist government. Whole villages, with their houses, yards, barns, stables, gardens, were erased. In their place stretched the open space of huge fields cultivated by tractors. I stood at the edge of a plateau above my river's canyonlike valley and saw only a plain without a trace of the clumps of trees that once marked the emplacement of every village. Among the many definitions of Communism, perhaps one would be the most apt: enemy of orchards. For the disappearance of villages and the remodeling of the terrain necessitated cutting down the orchards once

surrounding every house and hut. The idea of collective farming – grain factories instead of little peasant
lots – was rational, but with a vengeance, and a similar
vengeance lurking in practically every project of the
planned economy brought about the downfall of the
Soviet system.

Orchards under Communism had no chance, but
in all fairness let us concede they are antique by their
very nature. Only the passion of a gardener can delight
in growing a great variety of trees, each producing a
small crop of fruit whose taste pleases the gardener
himself and a few connoisseurs. Market laws favor a
few species that are easy to preserve and correspond
to basic standards. In the orchards planted by my
great-grandfather and renewed by his successors, I
knew the kinds of apples and pears whose very names
pronounced by me later sounded exotic.

I found myself in the spot, now marked by a clump
of weeds, where the house once stood. It was taken
apart in the fifties, and instead of a round lawn before
it, a tangled forest of young trees, mostly maples,
began, sloping down to the river. The lawn was nearly
impassable, as the old paths had disappeared in the
wild outgrowth. Here and there an aged oak or elm
survived. The orchards were gone, just of their old
age, to judge by the few dry stumps remaining.
Everything here had been abandoned for years, and

nobody seemed to make use of the land. In a haphazardly put together hut an old couple lived a squatters' life, and the only profit they drew from the estate was, I guess, the abundance of dry wood to feed their stove during the long northern winters.

I did not feel any regret, or anger, or even sadness. I was confronted not by the history of my century but by time itself. All the human beings who once walked here were dead, as were most of those anywhere on the earth born the same year as I. Granted the privilege of return, I was aware that it was only possible because a certain big empire had fallen, but what was most important at the moment was the tangible element of flowing time. I went down to my river. It had no lily pads and no calamus, and its reddish color confirmed the presence of chemical plants operated in its upper run. A lonely wild swan kept itself immobile in the middle of oily water, an incongruous sight, suggesting illness or the bird's suicidal intent.

The sky was clear, vegetation lush on that June day. I tried to grasp and name my feelings. My memory recognized the outline of hills on the other side of the river, the slope of the park, a meadow by the road, a dark shaded patch of greenery where once there was a pond. In spite of all the changes, the configuration of the terrain persisted, and it seemed to me I could have found my way even with closed eyes, for my feet would have carried me everywhere themselves.

Much was going on inside me, and I was stunned by the strength of that current for which no name seemed adequate. It was like waking up from a long dream and becoming again the person whom I have never ceased to be. Long life, narrow escapes, my two marriages, children, my failures and triumphs, all flickered as if telescoped into a film running at a great speed. No, this is not a proper description, for all that existed in a big lump separated from me, placed in its own dimension of the past, while I was recovering my continuity from myself as a child to myself as an old man.

In a world dominated by technology and mass mobility, most of us are first- or second-generation immigrants from the country to big cities. The theme of homeland, the whole nostalgic rhetoric of *patria* fed by literature since Odysseus journeyed to Ithaca, has been weakened if not forgotten. Returning to my river valley, I carried with me my heritage of these venerable clichés, already grown somewhat pale, and I was rather impervious to their sentimental appeal. Then something happened – and I must recognize that the myth of Ithaca stems from profound layers of human sensibility. I was looking at a meadow. Suddenly the realization came that during my years of wandering I had searched in vain for such a combination of leaves and flowers as was here and that I have been always yearning to return. Or, to be precise, I understood this after a huge wave of emotion had overwhelmed me, and the only name I can give it now would be – bliss.

Dictionary of Wilno Streets

Why should that city, defenseless and pure as the wedding necklace
    of a forgotten tribe, keep offering itself to me?

Like blue and red-brown seeds beaded in Tuzigoot in the copper
    desert seven centuries ago,

Where ocher rubbed into stone still waits for the brow and cheek-
    bone it would adorn, though for all that time there has been no
    one.

What evil in me, what pity, has made me deserve this offering?

It stands before me, ready, not even the smoke from one chimney is
    lacking, not one echo, when I step across the rivers that separate
    us.

Perhaps Anna and Dora Drużyno have called to me, three
    hundred miles inside Arizona, because except for me no one
    else knows that they ever lived.

They trot before me on Embankment Street, two gently born
    parakeets from Samogitia, and at night they unravel for me
    their spinster tresses of gray hair.

Czesław Miłosz

Here there is no earlier and no later; the seasons of the year and of the day are simultaneous.

At dawn shit-wagons leave town in long rows, and municipal employees at the gate collect the turnpike toll in leather bags.

Rattling their wheels, Courier and Speedy move against the current to Werki, and an oarsman shot down over England skiffs past, spread-eagled by his oars.

At St Peter and Paul's the angels lower their thick eyelids in a smile over a man who has indecent thoughts.

Bearded, in a wig, Mrs Sora Kłok sits at the counter, instructing her twelve shopgirls.

And all of German Street tosses into the air unfurled bolts of fabric, preparing itself for death and the conquest of Jerusalem.

Black and princely, an underground river knocks at cellars of the cathedral under the tomb of St Casimir the Young and under the half-charred oak logs in the hearth.

Carrying her servant's-basket on her shoulder, Barbara, dressed in mourning, returns from the Lithuanian Mass at St Nicholas to the Romers' house on Bakszta Street.

How it glitters! the snow on Three Crosses Hill and Bekiesz Hill, not to be melted by the breath of these brief lives.

And what do I know now, when I turn into Arsenal Street and open my eyes once more on a useless end of the world?

I was running, as the silks rustled, through room after room without stopping, for I believed in the existence of a last door.

*But the shape of lips and an apple and a flower pinned to a dress
were all that one was permitted to know and take away.*

*The Earth, neither compassionate nor evil, neither beautiful nor
atrocious, persisted, innocent, open to pain and desire.*

*And the gift was useless, if, later on, in the flarings of distant
nights, there was not less bitterness but more.*

*If I cannot so exhaust my life and their life that the bygone crying is
transformed, at last, into a harmony.*

Like a Noble Jan Dęgboróg *in Straszun's secondhand bookshop,
I am put to rest forever between two familiar names.*

*The castle tower above the leafy tumulus grows small and there is
still a hardly audible – is it Mozart's* Requiem? *– music.*

*In the immobile light I move my lips and perhaps I am even glad
not to find the desired word.*

Antokol

First one passed the dock. Iron barriers along the
sidewalk polished to a shine by the touch of hands;
you could lean against them, or sit and watch. If I am
to speak now about what one could see there, I should
first explain that I am there simultaneously as a small
boy and an adolescent and a young man, so that many
years of watching are concentrated in a single moment.
So, what one saw first of all was a boat preparing for

departure or, rather, the public boarding by means of a gangplank, the pressing of fingers into ears as the whistle sounds once and then again, the untying of the ropes with Józiuk shouting at Antuk and Antuk at Józiuk; or, a boat approaching, still far away when the shimmering of its wheels is first discerned. The boats were named *Courier*, possibly *Express* (although I am not sure about that); later on there was a third one, *Speedy*, a wonderful boat with a real deck. A lot depended on which one you happened to take during school outings to Werki. They went upstream, to Werki and even farther, to Niemenczyn – never downstream. There was also a dock for the small boats painted with stripes of many colors along their sides, from the slightly elevated prow to the stern. The ferryman would seat five or six people and cross over to the other shore, to the Pióromont district, using a long oar, also painted, punting, unless the water, in spring or late autumn, was high. One also watched the 'flats' floating by, long trains of floating timber, mainly pine, with a hut and a fire on the last raft, which also had an enormously long and heavy steering oar. The sawmills where the 'flats' tied up, so that sometimes the Wilia would be completely covered by them, were somewhat farther downstream, past the Green Bridge, across from St Jacob's.

I also knew larger boats – they were on the Niemen,

not the Wilia – from my visits to Kaunas. Almost like illustrations in travel books, they had decks loaded with crates and barrels; sometimes there were cows and horses, too. They went to distant places, as far as Jurbork. To tell the truth, the one I used to take was not large, because it went up the Niemen for only part of its route, to the mouth of the Niewiaża, and then it sailed up the Niewiaża to the town of Bobty. The Niewiaża is quite deep but very narrow and tortuous; it is navigable to that point, but not farther upstream. For some reason, I thought of the local boats as something official, like the post office, and I was surprised that their crews spoke among themselves in exactly the same sort of Polish as the crews of the *Speedy* and the *Courier*.

One always walked past the dock on the way to Antokol; that is why I'm speaking of it now. Then the bridge or, rather, the bridge across the Wilenka where it flows into the Wilia. Antokol itself is, first of all, the boredom of a long, only partly built-up street, a muscular memory in the legs, about a space 'in between': between the Wilia on the left and the hills on the right. Only the slopes of Castle Hill, in the angle formed by the Wilia and the Wilenka, were luxuriantly green, with the foliage of a deciduous, forest. Three Crosses Hill and the other hills were sandy inclines sparsely dotted with pines. We often went climbing there, for the view and the solitude, but basically it was too windswept a place, and the somewhat more distant, hilly Antokol, beyond St Peter and Paul's, was more interesting. I knew the Baroque statues of that church from photographs, and even from the postage stamps of Central Lithuania, but when I toured the interior I was disenchanted: a host of details obscured by whitewash, details so minuscule that they could be seen only with a magnifying glass. Beyond the church, deeply rutted, sandy roads wound through the forest; they had street names: Sunshine, Springtime, Forest, etc., with a few wooden houses concealed in the thickets, more like dachas than villas. In one of them lived Leopold Pac-Pomarnacki, my schoolmate and partner in my naturalist's passions: a phlegmatic elderly gentleman with a protruding belly, fourteen years of age. I was in awe of his collections of rare ornithological books and stuffed birds. An only child, the son of rather elderly parents, I think, he had his very own shotguns. An expedition with him to the country, to visit Nowicki, another schoolmate, whose face I remember but not his first name, remains in my memory as something exceptionally enigmatic, a tormenting darkness from which I am able to retrieve only one or another fragment that immediately disappears. It took place on All Souls' Day, somewhere on the southern boundary of the Rudnicka Wilderness, because it seems we got off the train at Stasily, beyond Jaszuny. Frozen earth, sunsets and sunrises that mixed reds and blues, hoarfrost, a hamlet, fried bliny at dawn, conversations in Belorussian, hunting, and staying by ourselves in a house that was, I think, the residuary part of an estate. There were four of us, one a girl, a student at a Wilno *gymnasium* or technical school – her black eyes, pallor, throaty laugh (but I have no image of her face) – and although Pac and I were complete outsiders here, Nowicki and she kept getting into ominous erotic brawls that excluded me, a mere puppy, from their partnership. During that same school year, in early spring, she was found dead in Zakret, in the German military cemetery – it was suicide, poison or a revolver, but not connected with Nowicki.

Next to St Peter and Paul's there were also some trails leading up to the ski slopes. An absolutely undeveloped highland, called Antokol Grove and Altaria on the city maps, extended all the way to the outskirts of Zarzecze and Belmont; the runs were mostly short and headlong. I skied like a cow, but for a brief period at the beginning of my university career and my ardent participation in the Vagabonds' Club, I did so stubbornly. It was the period of my friendship with Robespierre, who used to ski wearing a red flannel shirt, so for me the snow of the Antokol hills is fused with that shirt in a single image. But I remember the outskirts of Antokol, where the city ended and the highway to Niemenczyn began, because that is where as a child I observed the panic of the 1920 retreat.

Nevertheless, Antokol remains for me not so much streets which one walks on as a shore along which one sails: just beyond the bridge on the Wilenka were the rowing clubs, among them the AZS [Academic Sport Union], from whose landing we would push off in a kayak or canoe. The Wilia is a swift river and though we paddled energetically against the current, we could only glide quite slowly along the Antokol shore. Across from the AZS, on the opposite shore of the Wilia, was Pronaszko's Mickiewicz, a gigantic Cubist bloated figure, exiled there by the town fathers, who were probably right not to want to place it in the center of town among the old stones. There, too, all of a sudden, was the first sandy beach: Tuskulany. We were drawn to more distant places, so I was at that beach only once, while I was still a high school student playing hooky. It happens that, for no obvious reason, particular hours in my life have been preserved with absolute clarity about their details, so I can see the naked people lying there beside me. One of them is a future electrical engineer and officer in the Royal Air Force: Staś. Many years later (it is painful to count them), in 1967, the two of us camped on the shores of big Eagle Lake in the California Sierras, and when we headed straight from our tent to the water the moment we woke up, or went kayaking along its wild forested shores, we didn't look the way we did in Tuskulany; yet it was difficult for me to grasp how our bodies had changed – only perhaps that his wedge-shaped, Russian czar's beard had begun to turn gray.

In the names of the settlements along the Wilia one could discover amalgams of familiar and foreign words. Tuskulany, I assume, was named by enlightened readers of Latin literature who perceived similarities between this region and Tusculum, the country retreat of wealthy Romans. Wołokumpie is less refined. Trynopol, actually only a white church on a bluff, a sign to oarsmen that they can relax because the most treacherous currents are behind them, makes one think of Trinitas and thus has a derivation similar to that of nearby Kalwaria. Charming forested Werki reminds one of German Werk, but according to legend the name is derived from crying eagle chicks – in Lithuanian, *verkti* means to cry.

The Wilia alongside Antokol and all the way to Werki was our city's *freeway*, a word I learned much later, substituting it for the dubiously Polish word *autostrada*. Although I would prefer to say *gościniec* –

highroad. So, a highroad, down which the Wilno population would travel on a Sunday outing – the native population that had been living there for generations, which was neither gentry nor working-class but rather petit bourgeois and thus employed for the most part as artisans. On passenger ships or in small boats, in family groups: shirts, suspenders, taking turns at the oars, the women's colorful dresses, and a jar of pickles for a snack. Another popular amusement was the sauna. At the end of the week one could hear all sorts of idiosyncrasies of 'local' speech there, which would have been a treasure for linguists, although I doubt that linguists ever frequent public saunas.

Upstream from Werki, and almost never frequented by people on excursions, the Wilia remained virtually untouched by 'civilization.' I have preserved it in my memory from the point where the Żejmiana emptied into it. Absolute silence, only the splashing of water against the hull, in the sunshine the brilliant whiteness of the steep sandy bluffs with holes drilled into them by cliff swallows, the dangling roots of the pines. Occasionally, a long string of floating log rafts with smoke rising from a stove. There is a particular majesty in the slow turning of these 'flats' along the bend of a river. A steering oar in front, a steering oar in back, often plied by two people, a man and a woman, the long train of rafts gliding slowly into a new current. Occasionally a fishing boat would flash by in the other direction, toward the bank; sometimes there would be a naked lad in a kayak, who was probably spending his school vacation somewhere nearby, unaware of the devilish traps that History had already set for him.

In the summer the Wilia across from Antokol became shallow; sometimes it was possible to wander downstream for a couple of kilometers, swimming some of the time, but mostly touching the bottom. I associate the Wilia with Antokol because the sawmills beyond the Green Bridge signaled its end as a highroad. Farther on, the river headed for the closed Lithuanian border; besides which, it probably wasn't navigable, considering that in at least one spot it had whirlpools and rapids that were difficult to negotiate. The city's sewage, especially from the hospital in Zwierzyniec, made one loath to swim in the river near Zwierzyniec and also near the opposite shore, by the Zakret forest. Excursions downriver exposed one to an arduous return trip against the current and therefore were rarely organized. We took the train to the settlements of the Students' Union in Legaciszki, which were right on the Lithuanian border.

Arsenal Street

This is a short street, stretching from the corner of Embankment Street, just beside the boat dock, to Cathedral Square. In the olden days, it seems, it was simply the continuation of Antokol Street, its extension. A handful of houses along a single sidewalk; in place of a second sidewalk, the iron curves of a low palisade enclosing a garden (at the rear of the cathedral) that was called the Calf Pen. The corner of Embankment Street was occupied by a large, rather ugly building, the Tyszkiewicz Palace, which was always locked; later on, I learned that it housed the Wróblewski Library; its function derived from the fact that it existed and I never asked myself why. A few years before the war it was taken over to house the Institute for the Study of Eastern Europe and then I often had occasion to go to this building. On the other hand, from the time I was in the lowest *gymnasium* classes I paid regular visits to the house in the middle of Arsenal Street, at number 6, because my relatives lived there, distant relatives, to be sure: the Pawlikowskis. The blood tie was with her, Cesia Pawlikowska, *née* Sławińska, I think; she insisted that

I call her aunt. The man of the house, Przemysław Pawlikowski, was an ex-colonel of the czarist army; on the walls hung photographs from Bessarabia, where they had lived for a long time and apparently once owned an estate. Tall, swarthy, lean, taciturn, he walked about in a patterned bathrobe, sat on the balcony staring at the green of the garden, or played patience. He also worked on his stamp albums, which tantalized me, because of course I was caught up in this mania, and he would give me rare specimens as a gift. Of their two sons, I have no recollection of the first, Danek, who committed suicide as a young man; the second, an engineer, went to Soviet Turkestan after the war to work there as a specialist (a 'spets'), returned with a Russian wife, bought a car, and became one of the first taxi drivers in Wilno, an avant-garde profession – for who ever heard of a well-born man taking tips from a guest? His Russian wife wore Oriental *sharovary* at home and smoked cigarettes in a long cigarette holder. Wacek's sister, Marysia, worked in an office, and so that peaceful family collective (they all lived together) could serve as an illustration of the sociological changes that were taking place at the time. I met Marysia when I was a very young boy, because she stayed with my grandparents for a while in Szetejnie, in Kaunas, Lithuania, and it was she who read *With Fire and Sword* to me on the oilcloth couch near the window in the dining room, where you had to curl up in a hollow and guard the spot you had warmed up, not letting your bare feet protrude onto the cold oilcloth beside you. Marysia, as I think the old folks told me, was somewhat 'mannered'; for me, she was simply mysterious, introspective, pensive, swaying at the hips, tall; she wore a black velvet ribbon around her white neck. She belonged to the generation that came to maturity on the threshold of the First World War, which is why there were volumes of poetry and literary journals from that period in the house on Arsenal Street. If I had not examined the contents of those shelves, I would never have known, for example, that an almanac, *Żórawce*, was published in 1914 or 1915, filled with poetry and prose of late-period Young Poland. In general, my relatives, who were already grown-up young ladies, affected me somewhat erotically in my childhood, furnished me with an insight into an epoch that I could not remember; their style of living itself had preserved something from it. Today it strikes me as laughable to call those times, which then were only ten years in the past, another 'epoch,' for if those who were familiar with it seemed to me to have emerged from murky darkness, probably a general law was at work: for every generation the events, styles, and fashions that are just barely in the past are extremely distant. However, it is impossible to determine if that is always so and if, for example, the 1950s are another geological era for young people today. Certainly, the First World War and the independence of Poland were a watershed for Marysia and her generation, but not as significant a one as I thought them to be.

Marysia lived an office life, which meant not only work but also friendships, picnics with colleagues, even office excursions abroad. During those years when I used to visit them, first as a *gymnasium* student, then as a university student, she was beginning to age and I would think about how it is that women become old maids. At 6 Arsenal Street I felt at home, and because it would have been hard to find a more central location in the city, sometimes I dropped in there simply to stretch out on the sofa. I wrote a couple of poems there that I like to this day. Also, I spent my last night in Wilno in that apartment, before my journey which was more risky than I wanted to admit to myself, to Warsaw across the green border in 1940. This was shortly after the occupation of the city by Soviet troops, which was barely noticed by the family, because Uncle, Pawlikowski was dying and their main worry was buying bottles of oxygen.

The Institute for the Study of Eastern Europe, housed in the rebuilt or added-on part of the large corner building, was modernity, lots of light, brightly painted walls, furniture made from light-colored woods. Usually I would wait patiently while Dorek Bujnicki attended to the students at his little window, after which we showed each other our poems and dreamed up literary pranks. There was a Lithuanian who also used to hang around there – Pranas Ancewicz. We were close friends and there was a time when we saw each other every day, because we both lived in the Student House on Bouffałowa Hill. Now that I've mentioned his name, I cannot refrain from remarking that I know of very few people who have been slandered the way that wise and good man was. And no one knows better than I that it was all bare-faced lies.

The Institute is for me the period just before my departure for Paris and immediately after my return, 1934 and 1935, a period of dramas and intoxications, also of travels. Perhaps, aside from strictly personal causes, one might detect in this some sort of short-lived opening up in the whole country, between the chaos of the economic crisis and the gathering darkness of the end of the thirties, a soaring, along with, to be sure, a presentiment of the approaching terror. I received a literary fellowship to Paris. Nika, a woman I had met in the Institute and had become friendly with, went to Moscow on a fellowship. The first book of poems by Boris Pasternak that I read, *Vtoroe rozhdenie* [*Second Birth*], was a gift from her. Just about that time Pasternak traveled abroad for the last time, to Paris, to the Congress in Defense of Culture, but he was in a tenuous position and was no longer being published.

The entrance to the Calf Pen was directly across from Arsenal Street. I had all sorts of experiences along the boulevard that led to Royal Street, but there are no sentimental memories associated with this garden. Open to passersby like a public square, it was not considered a congenial place for conversation or for holding hands, because the sight of all the nannies and the soldiers crowded together on its benches cast something of a pall on the splendid repetitiveness of such occupations. Probably my most detailed memories of the garden's recesses are from my childhood, from daytime games, when it was still neglected and practically empty.

Bakszta Street

Never in my Wilno years did I stop to consider why this street bore this name. The word was vaguely associated with *baszta*, or tower, which is correct. Bakszta was a very old, dark, narrow street, with horrible ruts in the roadway, no wider than two or three meters in some spots, and with deep open gutters. As a child I was rather afraid to venture into it because it had a bad reputation: right after you turned onto Bakszta from Grand Street you passed a multistory building with white-painted windows – the hospital for venereal diseases. At the upper windows sat whores who were there for a compulsory cure, mocking the passersby and screaming ugly words. It is not because it was so widespread that prostitution in Wilno is worth paying attention to; this oldest of human professions shows no signs of disappearing anywhere, it just changes its form. In Wilno, prostitution maintained completely nineteenth-century forms or, rather, nineteenth-century-Russian forms, just as in Dostoevsky's novels. That is, the drinking bouts of officers and students in exclusively masculine company would end with trips 'to the girls,' to the numerous little brothels whose addresses were known by every cabby. On certain streets (especially those below Bakszta on the Wilenka River, such as Łotoczki Street, Safjaniki, etc.) creatures of the female sex would stand in front of the gates for hours, adapting to the rigors of the climate, so that in winter they wrapped themselves up in woolen scarves, wore thick felt boots or tall leather boots, and stamped their feet in the snow to keep warm. The reservoir for this working force, just as for servant girls, was the countryside or the wooden outskirts of the city, which were not too different from the village.

But, more than anything, Bakszta was Barbara. Here and there, especially from the direction of the hillsides and bluffs near the Wilenka, a pedestrian looking in through the gates would see large court-yards and gardens; one of these sprawling estates was the Romer House. If I am not mistaken, my first journey from Niewiaża to Wilno ended there, because we used horses, and the Romers' courtyard, outfitted with a stable and a carriage house, made a good stopping place. The journey was a long one, 120 kilometers, and its significance is not in the least diminished by the fact that later I learned to drive that same distance by car in an hour. That is why we stopped at the Romers'; I don't know what social ties there were between us. In any event, later, throughout my entire stay at the *gymnasium*, the Romer House was managed by Barbara, a major domo and a housekeeper. Barbara came from my part of the country, even somewhat deeper into Samogitia, from the environs of Krakinów, and she had once served as my grand-father's senior housekeeper; we preserved a certain intimacy on the basis of these ties, and Barbara frequently visited us on Foothills Street. Tall, erect, severe, thin-lipped, she looked like so many of those numerous dark-haired and dark-eyed Lithuanians. An old maid, a pious woman, and a fanatical Lithuanian – the older people in our household used to make fun of these traits of hers, but gently. In all of Wilno only one church, St Nicholas's, held Lithuanian Masses (that is, sermons and singing in that language) and naturally Barbara went to Mass only at St Nicholas's. Anyway most of the faithful there were servants. I used to smile when, many years later, I would listen to my Viennese–Parisian friends' stories about Czech towns under the Habsburg monarchy. Naturally, German was spoken there, and Czech was considered the language of the household servants. I knew that only too well, except that in our eastern region Polish took the place of German.

From what I am saying about Barbara it is not easy to make any inferences about the strength of my emotional attachment. However, her image has accompanied me on my wanderings across a couple of continents. There must be a reason for someone surviving this firmly in our imagination. I remember Barbara's 'lodgings' in Szetejnie, which were as severe as she was, and this undoubtedly long-dead person has remained for me one of the most important figures from my early childhood.

Since it was so close to the university, almost directly across from the corner of Grand and St John's Streets,

Bakszta played an important role in the students' lives, because that is where the Mensa was located. Not a dining room, not a cheap restaurant, not a cafeteria, not a canteen, not 'a place of collective eating,' but precisely: a *Mensa*. It was one of the Students' Union's chief undertakings; the free or reduced-priced dinner coupons served as a stake in the political struggles for power. A rather dingy, dark building, it apparently housed the seminarists' dormitory at one time; for many years it was the only dormitory in Wilno – before the second one, very modern, was built on Bouffałowa Hill. I never lived on Bakszta, but every now and then I ventured into its corridors, with their blackened and well-worn wooden floors, in order to visit my classmates. The smell of lye, naphtha, soapsuds, tobacco. A similar corridor, on the ground floor, led to the Mensa. I have only a hazy recollection of its tables, covered with stained tablecloths (or was it oilcloth?), but I can see very clearly the small cashier's table at the entrance where one bought tickets for individual dishes. Almost always they were sold by a little gnome with a withered face, wearing a fantastic floppy black bow instead of a tie: Gasiulis.* An 'eternal student,' an already legendary personality, because he was active in student organizations in prehistoric

* Executed by the Soviet authorities for tearing down official posters

times, perhaps even in 1922 or 1923. In the Vagabonds'
Club he was respected as an elder, as one of the
founders; it was from his era that certain songs
dated, quite obviously inspired by Kipling's *Jungle
Book*, which was idolized at that time. ('On a high hill
the baboons were dancing their wild dance.') Today
I think that Gasiulis, like all the members of the
Vagabonds' Club, was very much a *hippie*. Our wide
black berets with colorful tassels made fun of the
generally accepted head coverings. On the other hand,
his black ascot came straight out of the bohemia of
Young Poland, as did the cape of the popular city
scoutmaster: skinny, sad-faced Puciata. Despite his
pure Lithuanian surname, I don't think that Gasiulis
knew Lithuanian. At one time he had wandered
through various distant regions; perhaps he had even
lived for a while in Cracow or Poznań – I could never
find this out because the difference in generations
precluded familiarity with such a celebrated, even if
somewhat comic, figure.

Foundry Street

Foundry Street means walking downhill. Many a
time, innumerable times, over the course of many
years, because I usually lived in the newest part of the

city, beyond Zawalna and Wileńska Streets, and it was Foundry Street that led from there to Napoleon Square and beyond, to the university or to bustling Grand Street. A triumphal descent, the ecstasy of physical exertion, the happiness of long, almost dancing steps, or absolute despair, or else, probably most often, that spiritual state when the young organism rejoices in its own way, despite the delusions of its tormented imagination. The descent began at the building on the corner of Wileńska, where the meeting halls of the Professional Unions and other similar institutions were located. A colorful array of notices was posted there, announcing lectures and boxing matches; fans of these performances, mainly young Jews, used to gather in groups on the sidewalk. A little farther down, on the right, but not as far as the corner of Tatar Street, were a couple of apartment houses with balconies that meant nothing to me until the moment when I began to spend my spring evenings on one of them with Stanisław Stomma, abandoning myself to intellectual disputes accompanied by rosy sunsets. It was 1929, I was a student in the eighth class at the *gymnasium*; Stomma, I think, was a second-year student in the law faculty and also an older brother in our lodge – the conspiratorial group 'Pet.' 'Lodge' is an exaggeration, but I cannot think of our group or of the Vagabonds' Club, which

I joined shortly afterward, other than as the peculiar creations of Wilno, the city of Freemasonry. Just as during the period of Wilno University's preeminence, prior to 1830, when many of our city's luminaries belonged to the Masonic lodges and rumors about this circulated freely, although I found out how numerous were the Masons among us only many years later. Unfortunately, the right-wing press erred in ascribing to Masonry a decisive influence on the course of historical events.

So, with Stomma on a balcony above a ravine of a street that descended toward tree-lined squares. We argued about Petrazycki, into whose theory of law and morality Stomma was being initiated by a young professor, a fanatic Petrażyckyist, a certain Lande. Having heard about Petrażycki, I, in turn, began reading some of his writings. We also argued about Henri de Massis's book, which was quite popular then – *La Défense de l'Occident*. At the time I was devoting myself wholeheartedly to studying French in order to read French authors in the original. It was probably Stomma from whom I borrowed the Massis, and still, over thirty years later, in California, I appreciate his lending me that book. This does not mean that I was ever, then or now, attracted to the French nationalists, the heirs of the monarchy. One must admit, however, that they were the first to sound the alarm, alerting people to the presence of ergot, the black discoloration that had begun to contaminate thought and language. According to them, this disease would arise in Asia and spread to the European mentality through the intermediary of Germany in particular; after 1918, through Weimar Germany – Schopenhauerism, Hinduism, Buddhism, Spengler, Keyserling, etc. Massis and other defenders of the Cartesian trenches were unable to ward off the growing opaqueness of the French language under the influence of German philosophy, which, by the way, was not necessarily an import from the Orient. Who knows, perhaps my distaste for the 'wisdom of the East' that is sweeping California can be explained by the fact that I read those early warnings when I was seventeen years old.

Past the corner of Tatar Street, on the right, there was the open space of a plaza; on the left, some small shops, unremembered, and a restaurant or cafeteria that opened during the second half of my time at the university, where one got good-tasting dinners for 60 groszy. The owner was a Warsaw Jew, the clientele was made up of students, but for the most part they were not the same students whom one saw in the Mensa. Here I met my Jewish class-mates from the law faculty, who came mainly from Warsaw; Lithuanians and Belorussians also gathered here. I do not know why my memory has preserved only a few faces and names. One of them: my colleague Lerner.

A few more steps took one past the Church of the Bonifraters (the Brothers of the Order of St John the Divine). It was the lowest church in Wilno, and the church itself, plus the monastery buildings, which were also low, formed a kind of miniature fortress on a small square that was full of trees – lindens, I think. The Brothers ran some sort of charitable enterprise; at one time, they had an institution for the mentally ill, which is why if someone talked nonsense, we would say that he was fit for the Brothers. The church had two little towers, but in keeping with the nature of the whole building, they were mere curves, just two breasts on the building. The interior was like a crypt or grotto decorated in Baroque style, with a small spring-fed well more or less in the center of its elongated rectangular space. Miraculous healing properties were ascribed to the water from this spring; although its fame did not extend even to other parts of the city, its reputation continued to be useful within the parish. What was special about the Church of the Bonifraters was the way it gave one a sense of security, of the homeliness of divine-human affairs, of an impregnable shelter from the world. Later – after Poland – I had occasion to visit Eastern Orthodox churches, which are like little chests made of gold, or cells of beeswax, where the warm radiance of the walls, the smell of incense, and the liturgical songs have a hypnotic effect. No doubt this fulfills a human need for an enclosed, delineated space, subject to its own laws and fenced off from that other, limitless space. That was why I loved the Brothers; particularly at Easter, when people visited the 'tombs,' it would not do to pass by that church. If in the other churches Christ's tomb, displayed with more or less ingenuity, vanished beneath the high vaulted ceilings, was diminished in comparison with the altar and the columns, in the Church of the Brothers of the order of St John the Divine it was the central place, because everything there was practically on the same level as the floor. I almost forgot to add that Foundry Street turned into the Street of the Bonifraters near that small square.

German Street

Narrow and not too long, German Street was the most cosmopolitan of Wilno's streets, because the street that was supposed to be the main street was definitely not cosmopolitan. It was officially named St. George Boulevard at first, then Mickiewicz

Boulevard; less officially, it was known as St George Street, or Georgie for short. This thoroughfare, laid out with a straight edge and bordered by rows of apartment houses from the second half of the nineteenth century, did not elevate Wilno any higher than a provincial town, a Rennes or an Elizavetgrad, as I imagine it, where there must also have been a 'boulevard' for the officers' and students' *gulianie* [Russian for 'rowdy strolling,' i.e., carousing]. By contrast, German Street's cosmopolitan aspect was not diminished by its cobblestone roadway, which was repaved with bricks (as were all the important streets) only in the 1930s. As one approached German Street one left the underpopulated area behind and penetrated into a region of sudden density. Sidewalks, gates, doors, windows all sprouted multitudes of faces and seemed to bulge from the crowds. It seemed that on German Street every house concealed an infinite number of inhabitants who engaged in every possible trade. Beneath enormous painted signs, shop after shop fronted on the street, but the faces of lions, the pictures of stockings of monstrous proportions, of gloves and corsets, also advertised shops inside the courtyards, while the signs inside the gates gave information about dentists, seamstresses, hosiers, pleaters, shoemakers, and so forth. Trade also overflowed from the buildings into the roadway; it seethed around the pushcarts and the stalls erected at intervals in recesses along the sidewalks. Loaded carts, pulled by straining horses, thundered past. Touts circulated among the passersby; their job was to spot potential customers, praise their goods, and conduct those people they had managed to corral to a shop that often was located somewhere in a distant inner courtyard. I am positive that I never connected German Street with the illustrations in my French school texts that depicted nineteenth-century Paris; I arrived at that comparison slowly, only when I was already a resident of France. In the second half of our century, when it no longer exists, I have often thought about German Street, particularly when I wander about in the Marais district, staring at the signboards, especially since several of them practically beg to be remembered. For example, the one from the rue de Turenne on which to this day Monsieur Szatan recommends his tailoring establishment for men's suits.

German Street was exclusively Jewish, but it was significantly different from Warsaw's Nalewki, for example. More old-fashioned, more settled, it acted as the representative of a whole labyrinth of twisting, astonishingly narrow medieval alleys, and I never felt that hidden background in Warsaw. With its stones that bore the patina of time, Wilno's cosmopolitan fragments were probably closer to Paris than to Warsaw.

I visited German Street at various stages of my life, above all as a little boy accompanying Grandmother Miłosz. We were living in an apartment house at 5 Foothills Street, so we would walk down Foothills to the corner of Sierakowski Street, then along Port Street to Wileńska. Sierakowski Street demands a digression. At that time one could still see veterans of the 1863 Uprising; they wore uniforms and cornered hats, which were navy blue with a raspberry-colored rim. They received a modest pension, and even the widows of these veterans were not excluded, although of course it only amounted to pennies. Grandmother Miłosz also received such a pension. The street named after Sierakowski led to the Łukiszki district, to the square where the leader of the Uprising in Lithuania was hanged. My grandfather fought under Sierakowski in 1863, as his adjutant or officer for special commissions, I am not absolutely certain. In any event, he was a close collaborator and was saved, because in Serbiny, his family estate near Wędziagoła (north of Kaunas), he had as neighbors a village of Old Believers who liked him very much. The elders gathered and debated for an entire night over a by no means trivial problem: does a Christian have the right to swear a false oath in order to save a life? And they swore under oath that he had never left home throughout 1863.

From Foothills, across Sierakowski, then down port Street to Wileńska and German Streets – always to Sora Kłok's store. The store was in the courtyard, but it didn't need signs or touts; it was famous in the city and had a faithful clientele. It was well known that buttons, linings, wadding, and similar items such as no other shop carried could always be found there. I was fascinated by Mrs Sora Kłok herself – hideously ugly, fat, a faded redhead in a wig, with her goiter and her obviously shaved chin. She only commanded the troop of salesgirls; she was very imperious. From her store came the so-called tailor's supplements for my suits, which were either continually made over or sewn from homespun to leave room for growing. Shall I reveal the secret of habits I acquired in childhood? To this day a conditioned reflex takes over whenever I buy a suit: I'd better get it one size larger, because what if I should outgrow it?

After my boyhood years there is a big gap in my relations with German Street; I passed by there from time to time, and that's all. Only toward the end of my stay at the university did I begin to establish contact with it, attending guest performances of a Yiddish theater or visiting the little restaurants on its side streets with Pranas Ancewicz. The taste of chilled vodka and marvelous herring, but also the sensation of human warmth, dimly preserved in memory, guaranteed that I would always like Jewish restaurants. The jumble of side streets near German Street is worth mentioning, too, because that is where I sought out a rabbi in order to fulfill a certain errand. Namely, in 1933 or 1934 Oscar Miłosz sent me three copies of his little book from Paris; he had published it privately in a very small number of copies. Considering its contents, it is not at all surprising that he did not intend this work for sale. *L'Apocalypse de St Jean déchiffrée* – the book I'm talking about – prophesied catastrophes of cosmic dimensions that were supposed to strike humanity around the year 1944. It is possible, after all, that there were two pamphlets, not one – the other essay (either bound together with the first or separate) proposed the hypothesis that the most ancient fatherland of the Jews was located on the Iberian peninsula; and only there, and nowhere else, should one look for the biblical Eden. From this work, *Les Origines ibériques du peuple juif*, it appeared that the Jews are, most likely, the oldest autochthonous people of Europe. So, one copy was for me, and the others I was supposed to give to the (in my opinion) two most appropriate individuals – one a Christian and the other a Jew, if possible one of the 'illustrious rabbis.'

I selected Professor Marian Zdziechowski, because his pessimism about the future of Europe seemed to make him relatively open to gloomy prophecies. But I did not know Zdziechowski personally. As luck would have it, I approached him, stammering and blushing, on the steps of the university library, without having been properly introduced, and met with such an unresponsive welcome that it seems I didn't hand him the copy. Who the most famous rabbi was and on what grounds I selected him, I do not recall. I gave the copy to his secretary. I shall never know if it was read and if the author's intention – to issue a warning – was fulfilled.

L'Apocalypse de St Jean déchiffrée is a bibliophilic rarity, and my next adventure connected with this text took place many years after the death of Oscar Miłosz, in 1952, in the vicinity of the rue Vaugirard, where I was living at the time. I had run into Henry Miller in a small restaurant; I was astounded when I heard that he had been searching for this text for a long time. I promised to get him a copy, which wasn't at all difficult, since the Collection Doucet collects Miłosziana. I did not keep my promise and Miller excoriated me for that. Why didn't I keep it? It simply slipped my mind, but I suspect that the causes must have gone deeper than that and Miller rightly saw in it a reason to take offense. In my conversation with him I found his California catastrophism terribly distasteful: that's all we need, as if we don't have enough problems coping with the heritage of our European catastrophism. I detected intellectual chaos in what he said, and in his greediness for apocalyptic texts I saw a lust for sensationalism. So it cannot be ruled out that my resistance had a sacral character to it: I did not consider Miller to be one of the chosen to whom Oscar Miłosz had once wanted to issue his warning.

Wileńska

A street with a strange name, not homogeneous, changing form every dozen or so steps, ecumenical to boot, Catholic-Jewish. At its beginning (or end) at the Green Bridge, it was wide, lacking a distinctive consistency, for there were no more than a couple of apartment houses at the outlets of the various side streets; it constricted into a narrow throat beyond the intersection with St George (or Mickiewicz) Boulevard. When I was a child, the foundations of an unfinished building sat there for a long time, until at last a huge edifice was erected, a department store owned by the Jabłkowski brothers, the first more or less 'universal' store in Wilno, several stories high.

Not far from the Jabłkowskis', across from the Helios movie theater, was an amazing haberdashery, the likes of which I never saw anywhere else in the city. Its owners were not Jews but Poles from somewhere far away in Galicia, distinguished from ordinary people by their speech and their exaggerated politeness. The family: two women and a man, a family triangle, it seems. The man smelled of eau de cologne, his slightly curled hair was parted and combed smooth, his hands were white and puffy. They said, 'I kiss your hand.' And the shop did not remind one at all of what was normally meant by a 'shop'; the gleaming parquet floor was polished so that there wasn't a speck of dust on it; the goods were in glass cases.

Next door to this shop was a small bookstore, where every year on the first of September I experienced strong emotions, jostling against the other pupils and buying my new schoolbooks. Without a doubt, one of the most powerful experiences is to only look and touch for a moment, without knowing what is hidden under the colorful dust jackets.

Across the street, as I said before, was the Helios movie theater, remembered along with various films seen there, among them Pudovkin's *Storm Over Asia*, which made a powerful impression on me. But this theater also has remained in my memory as a symbol that evokes a vague feeling of disgust and shame that has been pushed away to a level deeper than consciousness. Among Witold's many unsuccessful careers (before he died of tuberculosis at age thirty-six) – his service in the Borderland Defense Corps, for example, his participation in a Jewish fur-trading cooperative, etc. – there was also an attempt at founding a cabaret review. The premiere took place in the hall of the Helios, and I, a fourteen-year-old boy at the time, was unable to defend myself with rational judgment against the bawdy vulgarity of this show; hence the shame – because of Witold, who, like it or not, belonged to the family, and also because of my parents, who even laughed – remained undiminished, spreading like a greasy stain.

On the same side of the street, right behind the movie theater, Rutski's bookstore was to serve as a kind of counterweight much later on. The son of the dignified, dour Mr Rutski was my colleague at the university and was married to Sitka Danecka; my relations with Sitka, before then, testify optimistically to the diversity of human relationships and the freedom from Form that is possible every now and then. We used to go on kayaking trips together, and we felt so comfortable with each other that we forgot about the difference in our sex. We were not, however, just 'colleagues'; we were linked by a much warmer mutual heartfelt caring. Nonetheless, no Form compelled us into erotic intimacies; friendship was more precious.

Beyond Halpern's shop (I think that was his name), where there was dust, semi-darkness, a wealth of dyes, pencils, paper in many colors, notebooks, Wileńska Street, now even narrower, turned into a street of Christian harness makers, cobblers, tailors; there was even a Turkish bakery. From it, or perhaps from another, came my *gymnasium* colleague Czebi-Ogły, who was a Muslim. Next, the façades of the buildings became subdivided into a multitude of little Jewish shops, and after a momentary rise in dignity across from the little square near the church of St Catherine (there was a beautiful old store there that carried hunting guns), Wileńska was dominated by impoverished trade all the way to the intersection of Trocka, Dominican, and German Streets.

From a courtyard on Wileńska, in its 'artisan' section, one entered a lending library to which Grandmother Miłosz had a subscription paid for out of her modest pension. I often turned up there, either delegated by her or to borrow books for myself, when I was twelve, thirteen. Mostly Żeromski, Rodziewiczówna, Szpyrkówna, that is to say, bad literature, and it seems to me that a tolerable intelligence in someone who received such training should not be underrated, with a few points added for the obstacles that he must have had to overcome. In all languages, *belles lettres* are predominantly kitsch and melodrama; however, the accidents of Polish history decreed that fiction had an exceptionally powerful effect on people's minds, as a language and as a sensibility, so that I suspect there is in the so-called Polish soul an exceptionally rich underpinning of kitsch. As for me – let's be frank: in the books that I borrowed from the library I was enchanted by such scenes as the death of the beautiful Helen in *Ashes*, who threw herself into a ravine, and perhaps even more so by the ending of a certain story that was translated from the French about the Chouans, or the counter-revolutionaries in the vendée. The hero's head is sliced off on the guillotine, but that does not put an end to his highly emotional adventures. To this day I can remember the last sentence: 'But his head, still rolling, whispered, "Amélie!"'

After All . . .

After all, I've done quite a lot of traveling. Partly of my own volition, but mainly as a result of circumstances which carried me about the world. Already as a high school student in Wilno I was trying to make order out of images of war and revolution in Russia; beyond that, everything was the future and a pledge that would never be redeemed. How many emotions I must have experienced, both good and bad, to have been, one after the other, in France, Italy, Switzerland, Belgium, Holland, Denmark, Sweden – I can't even count them, and then there's North and Central America. So I fulfilled, and then some, my adventurer father's dreams, although despite my romantic desires I never succeeded in assuming the role of a collector of places and countries, because life made too many demands on me. In any event, what at the beginning of the century might have seemed exotic was transformed with the passage of time into something universally familiar, in accord with an era of increasing motion.

My ancestors only rarely crossed the borders of their native Kiejdany district to visit one of our cities, either Wilno or Riga, but my father, even before Krasnoyarsk, had brought back from a journey through the Baltic region something of Europe in 1910, and leafing through the album about Holland, I would study the Amsterdam canals. Just as I studied his photograph, from 1913, taken on the deck of Fridtjof Nansen's steamship at the mouth of the Yenisei River.

There weren't many photographs in my childhood, and my imaginings about foreign countries were fed by a drawing or a woodcut – for example, the illustrations to Jules Verne's and Mayne Reid's books. But cinema had already come into play.

Many cities, many countries, and no habits of the cosmopolite; on the contrary, the timidity of a provincial. Once I had settled down in a city, I didn't like to venture beyond my own district and had to have the same view in front of my eyes every day. What this expressed was my fear of being broken down into my constituent parts, fear of losing my center, my spiritual home. But I would define this somewhat differently. We construct our private mythologies throughout our lives and those from the earliest years last the longest. The farther afield I was carried (and California, I'd say, is quite far), the more I sought a link with my former self, the one from Szetejnie and Wilno. That is how I explain my bond with the Polish language. That option seems lovely, patriotic, but in truth I was locking myself inside my own fortress and raising the drawbridges: let those others rage outside. My need for recognition – and who doesn't need it? – was not strong enough to lure me out of there and incline me to write in English. I felt called to something else.

My return after more than half a century to my birthplace and to Wilno was like a closing of the circle. I could appreciate the good fortune that had brought me such a rare encounter with my past, although the power and complexity of that experience were beyond my linguistic abilities. Perhaps I simply fell mute from an excess of emotion, and that is why I went back to expressing myself indirectly; that is, instead of speaking about myself, I started assembling a registry, as it were, of biographical sketches and events.

Miss Anna and Miss Dora

Miss Anna was short, almost a dwarf, with a huge head and a very ugly face in which the enormous wart on her nose was the most prominent feature. She carried out her profession as a teacher proudly and sternly; in her youth, it was a patriotic activity to teach the language which was looked at askance by the czars and to spread knowledge about the Polish Romantic poets. Many manor houses in Lithuania and Samogitia employed such teachers and the respect for Miss Anna in our family derived from her having been my father's teacher once upon a time. When independent Lithuania was formed in 1918, for a while Miss Anna carried out the duties of director of the Polish *gymnasium* in Poniewież. Later, however, during my student years, that is, she lived with her sister in Wilno, subsisting (poorly) on her meager savings.

She came from a backwater gentry family; she did not find a husband and became a teacher because there were very few ways for a single woman to earn money in those days. Miss Anna's spinsterhood embittered her and hardened her character traits, her resoluteness taken to the point of dictatorial rages, her easily triggered anger. She had no one, however, on whom to unload that anger other than her sister, Dora. Dora, who was certainly born to be married, also remained an old maid and had no one in the world other than Anna, whom she obeyed in every detail; she never insisted on her own opinion. Rather stupid, almost retarded, she fussed about her sister, doing the marketing, cooking, and cleaning.

They rented a room on Embankment Street and I used to visit them there, not quite sure why. It was one of my family obligations, like visiting relatives. These visits never took place without conflicting emotions: the sisters were from a long past era, they were old, poor, and helpless; my twentieth century, my youth, and my education made me superior, and from that came pity, empathy, and something like sorrow for the world, because human fates could turn out like that. I have never stopped seeing those two old women, defenseless against historical time, and simply time itself. No one but me remembers their names anymore.

Zygmunt Hertz

Zygmunt, a buzzing bee in search of the sweetness of life, and the demonism of great historic events: it is difficult to reconcile the one with the other. He grew up in Poland in the 1920s, when virtually nothing of what was to happen later seemed possible. He came from a respectable family and I assume that those who knew him before the war could see in him many character traits that were common to the spoiled only sons of patrician families. A handsome man, reasonably well-to-do, who ordered his clothing from fine tailors; an habitué of cafés and dance halls, sociable, popular, he probably had a reputation as a typical gilded youth, although his enlightened, well-educated father, a social worker in Łódź and also a bit of a littérateur, had infected him with a love of books. After completing his studies and his military service in an artillery academy, Zygmunt became an office worker in the Solvay firm, which sold caustic soda. He made a decent salary, bought automobiles, traveled, lived. He met a young woman who had recently completed her law studies and was already making a name for herself in a law firm, and he married her. Zosia was lovely and her beauty went hand in hand with exceptional virtues of character, which Zygmunt probably noticed immediately. He was quick-witted and impressionable, and, I think, had a thoroughly cheerful temperament, and thus he was free of any pangs of conscience because he had so many earthly goods and so much happiness and others did not. His skepticism and, as it were, innate liberalism protected him from both the profound soul-searching and the ideologies of our century. A private man by temperament and predilection, he shied away from politics.

When the two totalitarian states concluded the Ribbentrop-Molotov pact, replete with a clause about the division of the spoils, and unleashed the Second World War, Zygmunt was thirty-one years old. The division was carried out and as a result of the official slogan – *Nikakoi Pol'shi nikogda ne budet* [There will never again be any kind of a Poland] – roughly one and a half million Polish citizens were deported into the depths of Russia. Among them were Zygmunt and his wife, who were sent to fell timber in the Mari Autonomous Republic. His life as a lumberjack was to surface repeatedly in Zygmunt's conversation. The convoy of citizens of a state that had ceased to exist, sent off to the northern forests, came upon piles of wood that had been lying there for years due to lack of transportation and by now were rotted, like the already rotted remains of the Kuban Cossacks, the people who had chopped down that wood – which did not put the newcomers in too joyous a mood.

When I met Zygmunt in 1951, he had already lived through the exodus of Anders's army, Iran, Iraq, and the Italian campaign, after which the demobilized artillery lieutenant Hertz had attached himself to the three-man cooperative in Rome that founded the publishing house which was officially called the Instytut Literacki [Literary Institute] but was popularly known by the title of its journal, *Kultura* [Culture], and which was shortly afterward transferred to Maisons-Laffitte on the outskirts of Paris. Obviously, I have no intention of writing the history of *Kultura* here, but a few observations seem to be unavoidable.

Time is the enemy of our attempts at preserving reality, for it keeps piling new layers upon already existing layers, so that it is inevitable that we keep on projecting into the past. The great terror in Poland in 1951 already escapes our imagination, but it is easier to understand its causes than the phase through which the West European, or at least Parisian, spirit was then passing. This spirit, if we are to believe its pen-wielding spokesmen, was wallowing in existential melancholy because of its lost chance, that is, because the western part of the continent had been liberated by the wrong, read 'capitalist,' army. The few people who stammered out that maybe this was actually for the good were condemned as American agents, socially ostracized, and also dragged into the courts. The trial of David Rousset, a former prisoner of Hitler's concentration camps and author of the book *L'Univers concentrationnaire*, was being held at that time. He had the audacity to write somewhere that there are concentration camps in Russia, too; hence the trial for libel (I don't recall on what acrobatic legal foundation it was mounted) brought against him by *L'Humanité*. Under these conditions, the émigré journal *Kultura* was absolutely isolated; in other words, the situation bore no resemblance at all to the position of the émigrés after 1831, when the European spirit welcomed them as the defenders of freedom – which frequently counted for far more than the disapprobation of governments. In our century, only at the end of the fifties or, for good measure, only in the sixties, was there a lifting of the taboo, that is, a grudging admission that émigré journals are not necessarily the hangouts of scoundrels, fascists, and agents, and that one might even invite their contributors to one's home.

So there was Zygmunt in an unavoidably heroic situation simply because, despite his inclinations, he had done some instructive traveling and now could only shrug his shoulders at the buffoonery and disgrace of the European mind strolling along boulevard Saint-Germain. Also because while other old hands like him quietly busied themselves with making money in this West that wasn't, after all, the worst of all places, he had become a member of a cooperative that couldn't have been more obviously dedicated to impractical goals. Worse yet, he, such a private person, who so loved his own belongings and his own ways, had stumbled into a commune. This word has acquired so many meanings that perhaps it would be better to replace it with another word: *phalanstery*. This will not change the fact that *Kultura* was an insane undertaking that, for want of money, could exist only if its cooperative lived together, ate together, and worked together, giving to each according to his modest needs, no more. Zygmunt, I suspect, must have felt tempted to leave many a time. And considering his talent for getting along with people, his knowledge of languages, his energy, industriousness, he would have succeeded anywhere, in whatever he undertook to do. But he had made an emotional investment.

Wonder of wonders, that commune or phalanstery or *kolkhoz*, the *Kultura* community, was to endure for decades.

The beginnings of our friendship. That first *Kultura* house, a rented *pavillon*, immensely ugly and inconvenient, on the avenue Corneille; the cold of winter in the outskirts of Paris, with scant heat from the potbellied chaudières, loaded with coal; and that district of chestnut-tree-lined avenues that went on for kilometers, piles of dry leaves, and also something reminiscent of the nineteenth century in Tver or Sarajevo. It was there that Zygmunt became the witness of my by no means imaginary sufferings. And though someone may remark that it is his own fault if a humiliated man suffers, since he deserves punishment for his pride, still, the pain is not any the less.

I started writing *The Captive Mind* on avenue Corneille, but the simplest questions were missing from it, for I truly had no one whom I could ask them of. If, as long as I remained on the Communist side, I benefited not only from material but also from moral privileges, on what incomprehensible magic grounds had I, escaping from there, been transformed into an individual whom everyone considered suspect? After all, over there it was sufficient not to be with them one hundred percent, to publish a 'Moral [or dissident,

as we would now say] Treatise' and be engaged in
translating Shakespeare, to be considered a decent
man. And a second, or maybe the same, question:
Does an animal have the right to escape from a
forest that has changed ownership? 'The European
spirit had a ready-made opinion on this and it stood
guard with a double-barreled shotgun, that European
spirit incarnated in my Paris of Éluard, Aragon,
Neruda, with whom I used to share a drink not so
long ago. Because Zygmunt also knew about my
miserable financial situation and visa complications,
which caused me to be separated from my family for
three years, he considered my situation to be dreadful.
He watched over me tenderly, took care of me, and
whenever I went to the city he made sure that I had
a couple of francs for lunch and cigarettes. When I
accepted his offerings, I was too preoccupied with my
own troubles to value those gifts at the time, but I did
not forget about them, and for years afterward there
was a good deal of ordinary gratitude in my affection
for him.

Zygmunt was already a fatty at that time, but
vigorous, with a thickset body, healthy. A glutton, a
gourmand, a tippler, and above all a talker, the personi-
fication of jovial humor and a passion for sociability.
I say 'passion' because he seemed to have a built-in
radar that directed him unerringly to warm relations

with others, to laughter, gossip, anecdotes, stories. He could not have borne isolation. And he himself radiated such warmth that in the gloomy house on the avenue Corneille he would take the chill out of whatever the stoves could not warm up. He often irritated me with his excesses: he would keep popping into the study, its air thick with the smoke from my cigarettes, for I lived and wrote there, and just sit down and begin a conversation; his desire to do so was stronger than his decision not to get in the way.

'Czesiu, don't talk, you'll say something stupid. Write.' Zygmunt's advice, which I often repeated to myself later on, was very apt, and it referred to my bad habit of pronouncing extreme, offensive opinions out of spite. His advice was directed especially at my relations with *Kultura*, which at that time were not particularly harmonious. After all, we were creatures who were neither made nor molded in the same ways, and our meeting, at the intersection of different orbits, did not take place without friction, for which my provocations were chiefly responsible. Zygmunt, as his advice indicates, did not let himself be taken in, because he distinguished between my spoken and my written speech. He tolerated the former; the latter, he trusted.

I didn't treat Zygmunt as a friend at that time, as someone whom one chooses and with whom one is supposed to have an intellectual understanding. He was more like a classmate, assigned to us without our participation. I sought other partners for my talmudic hair-splitting. In my eyes Zygmunt was a preserved specimen of the prewar intelligentsia, who had been formed by *Wiadomości Literackie* [The Literary News], *Cyrulik* [The Barber], *Szpilki* [Pins], with a philosophy transmitted by Boy and Słonimski of 'The Weekly Chronicles,' while I was bent on breaking away from prewar Poland in both its manifestations – the liberal and the 'national.' And yet, as it turned out once again, intellectual friendships and loves often take a dramatic turn, while those other ones, founded on sympathies that are harder to grasp, are often more enduring. We were not standing still, after all; we were changing, Zygmunt and I, in a way that, I think, brought us closer.

Identity crises are thresholds in everyone's life on which we can smash ourselves to pieces. To know who one is, what role to adopt and in relation to which group of people, even a small group, how one is viewed by others: in all of this, one's profession plays a prominent, if not key, role. That is also why I have never advised individuals who were already immersed in certain professions to emigrate from Poland – especially not writers and actors. I myself, after all, had to change my profession and accept the fact that in the eyes of those who surrounded me I would be only a university professor. Before that came to pass, I had accumulated a good many interesting experiences. The obstacles aren't what's important here, although I was certainly hurt when a young Parisian author, who had been recommended to me as a translator, said outright that he would love to translate me, but if he did, he could publish nothing of his own because 'they' control the literary journals. Some years later I was overcome with hollow laughter when I learned that a famous Parisian publishing house had given my new book (*Native Realm*) to a Party writer from Warsaw to referee – which is better, to be sure, than the French police of the nineteenth century gathering information about émigrés in the czarist embassy. But let me not exaggerate the obstacles. In 1953 I represented France in the Prix Européen in Geneva, although the French jury surely knew that my manuscript was a translation from the Polish. It was success that terrified me, because that's when I realized that in writing for foreigners I did not know and could not know who I am, and that it was necessary to end my French career. These adventures could not but lower my aspirations. I chose my language, unknown in the world at large; that is, I chose the role of a poet of Vistulania, as Zygmunt called it.

In light of these adventures of mine, I can summarize

Zygmunt's great internal battles as I observed them; I came to feel more and more respect for him because of them. Those who have held in their hands the *Kultura* annuals and the books published by the Literary Institute, and those who will hold them in their hands in the future, ought to think for a moment about the kitchen pots, the preparation of breakfast, dinner, and supper by those same three or four individuals who were also responsible for editing, proofreading, and distribution, for washing up, for doing the shopping, fortunately an easy task in France, and should multiply the number of these and similar domestic tasks by the number of days, months, and years. And also think about string, about wrapping paper, about dragging, carrying, handing over the parcels at the post office. Zygmunt's identity crisis was not unrelated to his former self-indulgence; that is, to his unenthusiastic purging of his self-will. Had he had a taste for renunciation, were he an ideological fanatic, he could have entered more easily into the skin of a manager, a cook's assistant, a shipping clerk, and a porter. But his relations with ideas were always less than cordial. Absolutely polite, loyal, he opened up only to people, not to far-reaching intentions which were abstractions for him. Who should he have been, how did his acquaintances, and perhaps he himself, view him? The director of a large, smoothly functioning enterprise, several telephones on his desk, secretaries, conferences, and, at home in his villa, an infinitely generous, genial host, a patron of artists, a collector of *objets d'art*, a benefactor of orphanages and hospitals. Undoubtedly all this was within his grasp, only under the condition that he get started in good time. But in the meantime, year after year slipped away in packing, transporting the packages in a handcart to the Maisons-Laffitte station, loading them into the train, unloading them at the Gare Saint-Lazare, shopping, cooking, etc.

Only if a collective lasts long enough will it appear *ex post* as an idyll, on the strength of its very survival. As a matter of fact, its daily life is full of tensions between individuals, and since Zygmunt was sensitive to individuals, he often suffered greatly. For it is not easy to accept the modest place that somebody has to occupy in a collective, and although it is clear that somebody has to take on the jobs for the physically strongest, this demands no small amount of self-discipline. Zygmunt's struggles with himself, his search for solutions, and finally his acceptance of the identity of an almost anonymous worker – that is the substance of his mature years.

Again I must turn to the distortions introduced by time. If one were to believe the Warsaw press of the 1950s, *Kultura* was a powerful institution that was equipped by the Americans, almost the equivalent of

Free Europe, with the same number of personnel (everyone judges by his own situation) as is necessary in Poland to publish a journal and books. Visitors from Poland were astonished to discover that this picture had nothing in common with reality and was one more example of the fabrication of legends in which the creators of those legends themselves eventually begin to believe. But today, when *Kultura* has passed its thirtieth anniversary, the significance if not the image ascribed to *Kultura* at that time no longer looks like an exaggeration. For *Kultura* undoubtedly has exceeded in longevity and in influence everything that the Great Emigration achieved after 1831, and has its chapter in the history of Polish writing, or, quite simply, in the history of Poland. Lo and behold, Zygmunt the bee, buzzing today above otherworldly meadows, is a historical personage. Only, when he made his choice, he did not know he would become one. The whole undertaking could have fallen to pieces and vanished without a trace, or the uncertain, unpredictable political conditions in Europe could have put an end to such experiments.

Can fat people experience deep emotions? Zygmunt was a combination of delicacy and gluttony, emotional circumspection and hooting laughter. His abdomen continued to grow larger and he came to resemble Zagłoba. Marek Hłasko addressed him as 'Uncle.' But

Zagłoba's mouth probably wasn't shaped like his: very sensual and somehow infantile, prepared to accept a pacifier or a swig of aqua vitae, capricious and nervous. He was born a hedonist and he was governed by the pleasure principle. And he found an abundance of pleasure in this world. Thanks chiefly to him, the necessity of a communal kitchen at *Kultura* turned into delights of the table, into feasts, revelries, because there was no stinting on food at least. Guests – non-stop, from everywhere, from European countries, from Poland, from America – assuaged his passion for company, his enormous curiosity about faces, characters, biographies. The trips to Paris with the packages gave him the opportunity to meet with one person or another over a glass of wine, to talk and gossip and watch the crowd. So it was that by following his natural inclinations Zygmunt discovered his true calling and his talent. And when he discovered it, everything began to fall into a discernible pattern, the individual scattered pieces of the puzzle of predestination now fit together, and what at first had seemed resignation turned out to be the most ambitious of choices.

In brief, Zygmunt was a *philanthropos* by calling, a friend of people, and his ability to do good for people could have found no better application anywhere than in that peculiar zone 'between Poland and abroad.' Zygmunt lived and breathed Vistulania; he empathized, flew into a fury, rejoiced, felt ashamed because of what was going on over there, treated his involvement with it as an illness, but an incurable one, one that he had stopped struggling against. As was his wont, this constant worry over Poland always took on a concrete form: the level of earnings, prices, labor conditions, personal freedom or lack thereof; that is, the fate of real people whom he knew through their names or through a detailed, though imagined, knowledge of their daily life. An idea would suddenly pop into his head about active participation, about offering assistance. The list of people who owe their fellowships to Zygmunt, their foothold in Paris, their invitations abroad, would be enormous. He thrived on his intrigues, deliberated over his moves, whom to set in motion, whom to target through someone else – just as he tormented me for the longest time until I agreed to go see Jean Cassou, the director at that time of the Muśee d'Art Moderne, with a certain young female artist, who immediately seated herself on the Parisian potentate's desk (and was victorious). How many similar intrigues there were, telephone calls, urgings, reminders! It looked as if Zygmunt had said to himself one day: 'Here I am, no greater future awaits me, so let's do as much good as possible.' If I have not emphasized his participation in the political formation of *Kultura's* profile, it is because he was ruled by his sympathy, anger, pity, his wonder at the noble and revulsion at the base – that is to say, in him everything had its beginnings in an ethical reflex. And as he grew ethically, enlarging his personal field of activity, his role as inspirer, intermediary, superb public relations man in the service of independent thought grew apace, and in this way, it can be said without exaggeration, his presence transformed and humanized the house of *Kultura*.

A skeptic. He responded with disbelief to the possibility of reforming a system guarded by its neighbor's tanks. As for those whom he helped, he had few illusions and noticed the mark of pettiness on them, of habits acquired in the struggle of all against all for mere pennies. He did not doubt, however, that he would have been just like them and, who knows, would probably have done some swinish things like many of them if he lived there. Zygmunt was always delighted that he was living in France, but also that he was not dependent on anyone in that West from which he expected so little. The house of *Kultura* on the avenue de Poissy, already an institution, already affluent, with its large library and paintings by Polish artists, was like an island that had emerged from the swirling seas, between one cataclysm and the next, and Zygmunt the skeptic would often express the hope that he would not live to see the next cataclysm.

I weep for Zygmunt for extremely egotistical reasons. Is there anything one can have on this earth that is better than a few friends holding each other by the hand, who together create a circuit and feel the current running through it? For me, after my emigration from there to America in 1960, Paris was just such a little circle of friends, but it was Zygmunt above all who held us together, it was his current we felt most powerfully, and now, as in a dream, our hands reach toward each other's but cannot connect. So my point of reference eastward from California has lost its distinctness. One might also give a different interpretation to the feeling of emptiness that has suddenly descended on me. For two decades Zygmunt was my faithful correspondent. He lovingly practiced an art that has been virtually forgotten today; his letters were charming, brilliant, intelligent, sometimes so amusing that they set off spasms of laughter, although his macabre Warsaw humor was dominant. And from those letters I learned not only what was going on among our Paris friends but also all sorts of Warsaw gossip through which the daily life of Poland was revealed, because Zygmunt's ambition was to know everything – and if throughout such a long period of exile I somehow did not feel that I had ever left Poland, it was thanks to him most of all.

Very likely, we were linked by being mired in Vistulania, he through his passion to know, I through language, in ways that were as complicated in him as in me, *odi et amo*. I never noticed any snobbery in his eager socializing with artists and writers; he was, if I may say so, a natural kibitzer and guardian of the arts, which stemmed from his curiosity about this particular species of animal. He knew this species and good-naturedly observed the parade of hunchbacks as, with more or less grace, they toted their variously shaped humps around, usually tormented with grief that they were who they were and not somebody else. Zygmunt had an aphorism for this: every woman of easy virtue dreams about being a nun, every nun about being a woman of easy virtue; a tragic actor wants to make people laugh and a comedian wants to play Hamlet. If I complained, he would remind me of this as consolation. In any event, in his opinion I was good-looking for a hunchback, which is to say, he saw certain manifestations of normalcy in me. As a matter of fact, our friendship was consolidated outside literature, as it were. His grumbling about 'philosophizing' – in which he included my essays – didn't bother me in the slightest. I have written various things out of inner necessity, but not without an awareness of the merely relative significance of intellectual edifices, so that Zygmunt's voice, the voice of the average reader, no doubt alerted me to something there.

'Czesiu, write for people!' But what did Zygmunt mean by writing 'for people'? He thought *The Issa Valley* was my best book. Many of his letters exhorted me: 'When are you going to write about the Dukhobors?' Once, when I came to Maisons-Laffitte from America, as we sat around the table I talked about a Dukhobor ceremony that I had seen with my own eyes in the woods of British Columbia, and Zygmunt's love of comically unbelievable sights found this almost too satisfying. Instead of accommodating myself to Zygmunt's request, I again wrote some 'philosophizing,' *The Land of Ulro*, only to hear again, 'Why don't you write for people?' This was already the summer of 1979, after Zygmunt's operation, when he was growing weaker by the day. I didn't cite my poetry (perhaps too difficult?) in my defense, but asked him: 'What about my translation of the Psalms? Isn't that for people?' He thought for a moment. 'Yes,' he said, 'that is for people.'

What good are our triumphs and defeats if there is no one for them to warm or chill? Zygmunt was upset when things went badly for his friends and rejoiced when they went well. One of his last letters is exultant because Czapski's paintings had finally 'caught on' in the market, and in his old age he had begun to sell a lot of pictures. And now I can't help thinking that Zygmunt, who witnessed my triumphs and my miseries, was the first person I wanted to please with a report of some piece of good luck, as if I owed him this for worrying about me when I was down. Living as we do in a fluid, hurried civilization, in which titles, names, fames change with great rapidity, we learn to value personal ties, and when someone like Zygmunt passes away, it is immediately apparent that nothing counts if we have no one in whose presence we can weep or boast.

Zygmunt was never ill, and having made it to seventy in good health, he considered that an achievement in itself. I have to mention here a fairly recent dinner party at Jeleński's, at which Zygmunt, in contrast to the rest of the company who were drinking wine, drained a bottle of vodka all by himself. I took him to the Gare Saint-Lazare by taxi and he started up the steps, unsteady but in control. The next day I asked him why he'd done that. 'To test. If I can.' At the same time, however, he was stoically pondering the briefness of time and grieving, but not for himself. He was also thinking about what would happen to his collection of abominations for, incorrigible scoffer and perverse tease that he was, he had amassed a large collection of decorations for distinguished service, from various epochs, like the czarist medal

'*Za usmirenie polskogo miatezha*' ['For pacification of the Polish rebellion']. What Polish museum would be pleased by such a bequest?

He was balancing his accounts, then, when there was still no hint of illness. So I was not surprised by his letter from the hospital after he learned that he had a tumor and was awaiting surgery. I have no intention of exploiting his correspondence; it is private. I will only permit myself to quote from this particular hospital letter, dated July 22, 1979:

Affairs in our fatherland are *non existing*.* For the time being, calm. Very little is happening. From the perspective of the operation somehow in the course of a few days everything has assumed the size of dwarfs. Mentally, I feel terrific. I have lived for 71 years, up till 1939 in luxury considering conditions in Poland – before I was 31 years old I had managed to own 3 automobiles, then that *drôle de guerre*, what can I say, you know those times that have continued to this day.

True: from 1939, the kolkhoz. At my uncle's in Stanisławów, in the Mari Autonomous Soviet Socialist Republic, in the army, then *Kultura* for the last 32 years. I have met hundreds of interesting people, whom I would never have known even had I been not a bureaucrat but the director of Solvay. I have never done anything truly swinish to anyone. I have

*'*Non existing*' in English in the original.

been quite useful, I have rendered crucial service to a couple of people, there is a small group of people whom I can count on. So what's the problem? I will not go down in the history of literature as you will. So what? I have no qualifications. You will go down, but so what?

I'm holding up as well as before and I hope that I will remain in good shape until the end. I'm even amazed, because it turns out that I have 'character'; that's blatant nonsense, I don't. Most likely in painful situations like this some kind of whalebones materialize to keep a man stiff, or else the whalebones disappear and a man is turned into jelly. I am fortunate that the former eventuality came into play.

Not everything had lost importance for him: 'the most essential thing' was his thoughts about his wife. Opposed to all melancholy, he comforted himself immediately: 'But then, why should I kick the bucket? After all, it's not inevitable.'

And just think, in his hospital bed, as always, he was planning his jolly prankster's tricks: 'Should worse come to worst, a bit of mischief. I shall request, not I, but it's already been arranged for here in Paris, that Paweł Hertz will place an obituary notice in *Życie Warszawy* [Warsaw Life] and order a Mass at St Martin's. I won't learn who "was sick," "was out of town," "had business obligations." It will be a riot.'

There is something terribly upsetting in writing about dead friends: one subject used to associate with another subject, and although his understanding of the secret of the other's personality was incomplete, and frequently replaced by an 'objectifying' glance, still, it was an exchange, every judgment remained, open to correction. But then all of a sudden: an object. And the embarrassing incompleteness of a description of an individual human being from the outside, the usurpation of divine vision, or, quite simply, a totalitarian intervention, as this unique being is subsumed under 'the universal,' 'the typical.' That's where the falsity of literature lies, literature that supposedly depicts man 'from the center' but actually constructs him so that a whole will be pieced together, subject to the law of form. There is nothing to hide. I have Zygmunt's portrait in front of me instead of Zygmunt, and I am piecing together details that are supposed to represent him, leaving room for only an insignificant number of contradictory details. A rare thing: to live one's life as a good and honorable man. Because I understand that this is a rarity, the demands of construction guide my pen. But the most important thing for me is what remains of Zygmunt's subjectivity, of his appetite, the greed with which he would toss back a glass of whiskey, his jokes, intrigues, pranks: all the motion, the incompleteness, the change through which, imperceptibly for him and for others, his destiny was being fulfilled – for who among us ever expected that from a distance Zygmunt would begin to look like a statue?

Pity

In the ninth decade of my life, the feeling which rises in me is pity, useless. A multitude, an immense number of faces, shapes, fates of particular beings, and a sort of merging with them from inside, but at the same time my awareness that I will not find anymore the means to offer a home in my poems to these guests of mine, for it is too late. I think also that, could I start anew, every poem of mine would have been a biography or a portrait of a particular person, or, in fact, a lament over his or her destiny.

Letter to Jerzy Andrzejewski

Dear Jerzy,

Doubt is a noble thing. I believe that if there were a recurrence of the biblical experience of Sodom, it would be necessary to seek the righteous among those who profess doubt rather than among believers. And yet, as you know, doubt is traditionally bathed in a glow and accorded dignity solely because it serves the seekers of truth as a weapon. Indeed, the most fervent people are doubters. Allow me, then, to take both sides, and do not think that when I speak as one who knows with a certainty, I do not also doubt; do not think, either, that when I doubt I am not also sensing right beside me, close enough to touch them, definite, indisputable things. Just as human sight is capable of taking in only one side of an apple, human speech cannot encompass any phenomenon in its total roundness. The other side always remains in shadow. You summon me to assist in the struggle against armies of the most varied moral laws, armies equipped with swastikas, hammers and sickles, portable shrines, banners. Each of them insists that only its system of values is salutary, appropriate, useful. Each of them rushes around the world, exhorting people to join its ranks. Looking at this variety of mutually contradictory laws, you ask what is it that could convince you that your own intuition will not lead you astray; you ask about criteria, about guidelines. You ask, won't this stage be subject to constant change in response to particular social conditions, to a person's origins and upbringing, and if that is the case, can that constantly shifting line, that function of the most diverse factors, be the standard by which the currents and ideas creating contemporary history should be measured?

Yes, this is a vague, uncertain foundation, so vague and uncertain that it is easy to doubt its existence. All it takes is to raise one human generation in a new, changed way, instilling in it a different good and a different evil, and what a dozen years ago would have elicited universal indignation will elicit universal praise. The elasticity of human nature appears to have no limits; indeed, our own age is an age of monstrous experiences which prove this alleged truth clearly and persuasively. But still I must console you. Attempting to appeal to that nebulous element, the kernel of common sense in man, is nothing new, by any means; it is not like the discovery of a new continent. On the contrary, it is as old as the world, or, at any rate, as old as culture that can be traced back to ancient Greece. This element has been known by a great variety of names throughout history. Depending on the epoch, and on intellectual and linguistic development, it has been called reason, *daimonion*, common sense, the categorical imperative, the moral instinct. And although different faiths and different laws prevailed, enforced by the might of the sword, more than one Socrates drank poison in the name of that vague, wondrously indefinable voice, more than one humanist was burned at the stake. Only yesterday, Aldous Huxley, whose *Jesting Pilate* is such depressing, unpleasant reading (since it reveals the weakness of the West), that skeptical Huxley took a trip around the world in search of verities, and in this summary of the results of his journey he states that although almost all his convictions were demolished as a consequence of his contact with the immense variety of human beliefs, passions, and customs, still, he was able to preserve one conviction. That one conviction was his belief in the similarity of human nature, irrespective of race, religion, and language, his belief in the identical moral sense and similar definition of good and evil, be it in Europe or

China or the Polynesian islands. Could it be that people like Huxley were the last, unworthy heirs of the European tradition? Could it be that their judgment was the last of the old world's delusions, a weak and deformed reflection of the final wave of humanism? And that in that case one ought to look at the extermination of people in camps, in prisons, with new eyes – look at it as a battle between red ants and black ants, without recognizing either the one or the other as in the right but rather granting that both species are right? Or perhaps we should instead admit that some human right, some fulfillment of moral law belongs to one side and that their perse-cutors do not share that right. But if we take that position, we return to the vague kernel of ethical intuition; verily, this is not something that has long since been put to rest, that should have been consigned by now to oblivion.

At this point in my argument, I am overcome with shame. I bow my head in sorrow over my own ten-dencies, which prod me toward a greater zealousness than I desire. It is enough for me to loosen the reins a bit, and I begin to pontificate in the manner of a prophet or preacher . . . Knowing how easily I lapse into exaltation, I fear that I will soon mention the devil who summons people to Mass by ringing his tail. I have very few qualifications to be a bard. So let us quickly extinguish exaltation with renewed doubt; let us return to bitter, scathing questions.

Over the last few years, observing the spectacle in which we all are also actors, I have been astonished – no less, I am sure, than you – by the plasticity of human nature. That man can endure relatively easily the loss of his property, of his family, his beloved profession, is not what I find most astonishing. That he grows accustomed to hunger, to cold, to being beaten about the face and kicked also fits within the boundaries of the understandable. But beyond that stretches a dark expanse of wonders, as yet un-suspected perspectives. Let us take the question of one's relationship to death. In so-called normal times (and perhaps ours actually are normal) death is surrounded by a ritual of magic gestures, incan-tations, and rites. The smell of death makes the neck hair of animals stand on end, but humankind drowns out the terror with the beating of tom-toms, the sound of organs, and the singing of mournful songs. Until recently, in Belorussia women mourners still keened over fresh graves. These rites give death the character of a singular event, the appearance of a phenomenon that disturbs the natural order; they make of death an event that is utterly specific, seemingly unrepeatable. As far as I can recall from my reading of the scholarly literature on this matter, the idea that death is inevitable is alien to primitive tribes – they ascribe death, if it is not the result of being eaten by wild beasts or being killed during warfare, to the influence of evil spells. Perhaps this, too, testifies to a ceremonious attitude toward death (if I may call it that). It is a different matter when, as today, new ideas are being born – for example, the idea of the mass extermination of people, akin to the extermination of bedbugs or flies. There is no longer any place for ceremoniousness. After a while these striking changes penetrate the psyche of the masses, who daily confront this phenomenon. A person lived, spoke, thought, felt. Then, the next day he's gone. (*'Jego voobshche nigde net'* – 'In general, he's nowhere,' as a certain Bolshevik told me when I asked him about the fate of Bruno Jasieński.) Death makes no more of an impression than the drowning of an ant makes on its comrades parading beside it on the tabletop. A certain insectivity of life and death, as I'd like to call it, is created. I suspect that we are beginning to look at man partly as a living piece of meat with tufts of hair on his head and his sexual organs, partly as an amusing toy that speaks, moves – but all one has to do is raise one's hand and squeeze the trigger and an ordinary object is lying in the same place, as inert as wood and stone. Who knows, perhaps this is the path to absolute indifference, including indifference to one's own death. It may happen that with good training and appropriate schooling people will die easily, from a lack of desire; they will treat dying as almost an everyday activity, between two shots of vodka and a cigarette that they won't get to smoke.

In any event, this will certainly lead to indifference to the death of others and to a change in the classification of murder as an ugly deed. Causing someone's death is dissociated from the reek of demonism, pangs of conscience, and similar accessories of Shakespearean drama. Young men in perfectly clean uniforms can then shoot people while gnawing on a ham sandwich. Yet another novelty is connected with this: criminal law, paralleling the ethical feeling of civilized societies, has linked punishment to the fact of guilt. Because X is guilty, X must die, or must be placed behind bars. Today the issue of guilt is fading into the background, and how pernicious or dispensable a given individual may be in relation to society has emerged in the foreground. X dies, even though he did nothing bad; he dies because his hair color, the shape of his nose, or his parents' background is considered a sufficient sign of his perniciousness. And it is difficult to cry out that this is happening outside the law, that these discoveries of a destructive war are the same as collective responsibility. On the contrary, the development of criminal law is clearly moving in this direction; the German and Russian criminal codes are symptomatic (see their definition of crime).

Down the road lie unequal rights and unequal obligations. For some one hundred years the democracies of the West have held to the conviction that all people are equal under the sun and should be judged according to the same principles – which in practice came down to a glaring inequality, depending on the amount of property people owned. The Middle Ages knew a strict caste system, which was gradually tempered by modern mores. The murder of a knight was not the same then as the murder of a merchant or a peasant, although genuine religiosity placed certain limitations on that disparity. In Sparta, as Taine reports, youths who trained for battle in camps would come out onto the roads at night in order to kill a couple of late-returning helots from time to time, for the experience and to prove that they had mastered the soldier's trade.

Today, the same differentiation is surfacing again, the same inequality of obligations and privileges. The claim that the democratic concept of equality is a definite model and ideal, and that what we see around us is a distortion and perversion, is therefore, at the very least, a doubtful proposition. To choose among the ebb and flow of the most varied aspirations of human mores, to take one period (and a rather short one, at that) as a model, and to condemn others – is that not a gross error, yet another error of untroubled evolutionism and faith in Progress?

Take the problem of freedom of thought. True, there have been periods when freedom of thought was placed very high, making it one of the hallmarks of man. But those years (from the start of the Renaissance, shall we say, until the end of the nineteenth century) are not particularly binding on us. Excellent educational results (and despite everything, we must include among them results that the Soviet Union can boast of) were achieved by the total elimination of independent thinking, and it turned out that people can get along quite well without freedom of thought. The question can also arise whether with the development of such technological means of communication as radio, film, and the daily press, freedom of thought is possible at all. Does this not mean constant infection with whatever ideas are in circulation, and even that when the masses are given ostensible freedom they may succumb to total unification?

Evidently, human plasticity is great and the search for constants, for an 'eternal man,' might turn out to be a risky undertaking. It does not seem to me, however, that this plasticity is limitless. It gives one pause that even the most incompatible moral-political systems appeal to the same elements in man and, independently of the various forms assumed by whatever ethical currents are in circulation, they make use of a similar ethical judgment. The call to heroism and sacrifice, whether in the name of the German people or the Socialist fatherland of the working people, incorporates a scheme that is in no way different from the praise of patriotism and masculine courage in Plato's time. The propaganda of the various fascisms rolls out images of a 'new order,' in which, in contra-distinction to the former democratic lack of order, people will be able to live happily, without fear of unemployment, wars, and economic pressure, that product of 'Judaeo-plutocracy.' The working people will be surrounded by care, mothers will have better conditions than in societies based on respect for money, and participation in the universal wellbeing and harmony will be shared among the people according to their deserts.

The falsehood of such assurances does not alter the fact that they appeal to the sense of rightness, to the thirst for justice in man. Propaganda devotes a great deal of effort to creating in soldiers faith in a 'just cause,' and the execution and torture of 'worse' peoples has been given an equally broad justification.

These are not merely enemies – for enemies the chivalric code, so highly valued in Germany, demands a certain respect. These are enemies of the human race, subhumans, and as such they are released from the prescriptions of ethics. Photographs of Poles, Jews, or Soviet commissars, appropriately retouched, are supposed to convince the viewer of the fundamental difference of these creatures, to inculcate faith in their inferiority. The principles of honor and ethics remain in place, but, as we know, they always apply only to relations among people. Certain groups of people are bracketed out, and from then on it is permissible to condemn them without breaking these noble commandments in any way. The presentation of the Germans as a people who have been wronged and hemmed in until now. – oh, those hastily unearthed strata of *ressentiment* – is no different than the depiction of the proletariat as an oppressed class, which at long last is meting out justice. I dare say, too, that the moral sense as a motor force is very much alive both in Fascism and in Communism, and that when we observe the monstrous things they do in practice, we should ascribe them not so much to the disappearance of all ethical brakes as to a change in motivation. This means that within those various armies that carry around the swastika, the hammer and sickle, portable shrines, and banners, there is one and the same ethical scheme, and that only its being filled with various contents is what gives these varying results. One can compare this to an algebraic model: depending on the values assigned to the symbols in an equation, various combinations are possible. National Socialism praises fraternity, collegiality, righteousness, nobility in relations between people, only 'people' here means Germans, and, more exactly, good Germans who follow their Führer's commands. The French newspapers, which have lately been trumpeting the ideology of 'national revolution' with a significant dose of cynicism, have been competing with each other in elaborating images of the nobility and beauty of the 'new order.' Lies like that are extremely comforting. The person who lies demonstrates that he recognizes a fictitious image as more alluring than reality. Indeed, propaganda is perhaps nothing but an appeal to man's instinctual sense of what ought to be – a perverse appeal, to be sure, which falsifies innate proportions. And although from time to time in the speeches of Fascist men of state an open confession of crime can be heard that makes the blood run cold in our veins, the majority of their statements are lies, sentimental appeals to God to bestow His blessings, and the rending of garments over the other side's lack of morality. This demonstrates that Machiavelli's prescription is immortal and that a ruler would be acting badly if he appealed exclusively to man's basest urges. On the contrary, while doing evil, he must robe himself in the toga of a benefactor of humanity, a savior, one who exacts vengeance for injuries – a precept that today's pupils of Machiavelli are following quite faithfully on the whole. Yes, yes, this is all as old as the earth, this is all known and undoubtedly only the absence of a necessary distance places in our mouths a sentence about man's total plasticity, the total novelty of what is being played out in front of our eyes.

Since we agree that even in the seemingly most predatory armies and programs an elementary ethical sense is surrounded with a certain degree of deference, we confront another problem. That same ethical scheme, that same sympathy for the good and disinclination toward evil lead to such varied deeds and are filled with such varied contents! The hierarchy of ethical values is easily overturned and its ranks reassembled. A German, a model son, husband, loving father of a family, will torment a subhuman, a Jew or a Soviet soldier, because he is obsessed with his vision of duty and justice, which commands him to cleanse Europe of similar vermin. The fact that a characteristic dose of sadism is added to the mix still does not undermine my example. A purely bestial sadism, naked and plain, occurs much more rarely than motivated sadism, equipped with all the arguments needed to make it into a noble and positive inclination. Jews and Bolsheviks are responsible for the war, they are harmful, they murdered Germans, they are subhumans, they are filthy, they belong to the lowest race, which is incapable of culture – rationalizations like these come to the aid of sadism, the beast that slumbers in every man, when it feels like going on a rampage with impunity – with impunity, which is to say, on the margins of the ethically ordered rest of his life, leaving him clean hands that can stroke a child's head or light the candles on the tree on Christmas Eve. What contents, then, should we use to flesh out a structure for an ethical norm, what should it be aimed at if it is not to lead us into depravity? Does a single true content exist while others are a counterfeit and a fraud? Contrary to all those powerful slogans of historicism, which denies that there are immutable, constant elements, I believe that one such element does exist. Every serious Christian will have no trouble agreeing with me, since the one eternally binding truth of the Gospels does not permit any deviations or sophistry. I said in my previous letter that I am searching for a reliable foundation apart from any faith and that I see that foundation in the ethical instinct – or whatever one might like to call it; that is the sole example in a vortex of dubious things. And now here I am, all confused. How can it be, one might ask, if that same ethical drive without which it is impossible, in general, to build civilization, at one time justifies slavery, then again lauds the burning of sorcerers at the stake or the slaughter of tens of thousands of Albigensians, and on another occasion is perfectly comfortable accepting the extermination of non-German peoples – can one accept that as a higher instance, as a model for deeds and ideas?! It is, perhaps, only an innate drive to assign value, but *how* to make those distinctions remains an open question, and once again we are deprived of any fixed point.

Here we touch upon the fundamental argument that has been going on for centuries in the bosom of Western civilization between the pessimistic and optimistic conceptions of man. Christianity has not looked with confidence upon man's innate capacity to distinguish between good and evil. The virtue of the Stoics, which existed without divine assistance, sinned in Christianity's view by an excess of pride. Human beings' innate inclinations, if not illuminated by the light of grace, could lead, in the opinion of the Church, solely to sin, blindness, and error. In addition, the Western Church looked with a certain amount of disbelief upon the earning of that grace in isolation, upon the settling of accounts between God and a human soul within the privacy conferred by four walls. *Ecclesia* was to be the intermediary, the dispenser of grace by means of the sacraments created for that purpose. And although human reason was not actually surrounded with contempt, reason had always to follow the path of God's law; reason – to use the language of the Church doctors – had to be illuminated by the sun of supernatural knowledge. This lack of confidence in man's possession of common sense, this reliance not on the average person's intuition but on the opinion of *Ecclesiae militantis*, expresses a pessimistic view of human nature as marred by original sin and incapable of distinguishing between good and evil without resorting to extraordinary means. The Renaissance and Reformation were acts of faith in autonomous morality, in the grain of truth within each person; they applauded natural reason. The bonds of the Church organization and the assistance of the sacraments were unnecessary since each human being possesses a voice which dictates unerringly what he should do and what he should not do. Grace and damnation became a mystery of the human heart, for which no priest can offer relief nor any encyclical simplify the path. That was the germ of faith in man as the judge of his own actions; that is how man grows to colossal proportions: master of his own destiny, answering for it only and exclusively to God. And then along comes that optimist Rousseau, reared in the Protestant spirit, and he proclaims man's natural goodness, paints in the most exuberant colors all the innate drives of the human animal, accusing civilization of perverting them. Next comes the optimist and Protestant Nietzsche, summoning man to total liberation from the chains of 'slave morality,' inciting, to a transformation of civilization in the spirit of power and health, but not truth, and pronouncing the slogan 'Let truth die, let life triumph!' (And so it did, poor, mad philologist.) Nietzsche is seconded by the Protestant and optimist Gide, his ardent admirer. And then these new men come along, these ultra-moderns, these worshippers of the magnificent beast in man, whom we know so well. I have a book by a young Nazi poet, presented to me by the author in 1935. I pick it up and read the dedication: *'Au dessus de la loi le Créateur a posé la vie'* ['The Creator placed life above law']. Yes, we know it; that's the way it is. Life is superior to law, life fashions and creates laws for its own purposes, life breaks laws when it needs to, and life is man – magnificent, not answerable to any court of law, free, deriving from himself the rules governing his conduct.

Slow down, slow down. I am too incensed. More than one Catholic writer speaks of Protestantism like this; we need only mention Maritain. This is the way

Naphta would have phrased it had his quarrel with Settembrini, inscribed in the pages of Mann's *Magic Mountain*, flared up again today. Faith in man has had some fine representatives, however, who, wary of Rousseau's and Nietzsche's perverse excesses, were measured in their claims and drew entirely different conclusions from their optimistic conception of man. I need only mention Anglo-Saxon literature as an example. Nevertheless, I must admit that whoever wishes to seek moral authority in man and to base himself on it, whoever believes in man's right to an autonomous resolution of ethical problems, is taking the path of Humanism and the Reformation and not the path of the Catholic Church. The path that leads from Luther to Rosenberg, as you correctly say, is by no means crooked, while Rosenberg is separated from Catholicism by an abyss.

No, I harbor no illusions. All noble humanitarians, debating to the present day the rights of man and of the citizen, are descended from the same spiritual family that the Church has condemned on many occasions, thus giving proof of the Church's wisdom. And just as the germ of monarchism and totalitarianism persists within democracy, so a germ of slavery persists in their appeals to complete freedom of conscience and thought. Man became free, but being free, he created certain historical ideas and bent his neck under the yoke which he himself had created. Soon the idea of self-sufficient humanity took hold. It was contaminated by the corrosive acids of the work of philosophers whose goal it was to prove that 'man' is an abstraction, that 'Man' with a capital *M* does not exist, that there are only tribes, classes, various civilizations, various laws, and various customs, that history is filled with the struggle of human groups, and that each of them brings along different ethics, different customs, and a different worldview. Like Marx, they yearned to prove that 'being defines consciousness' or, as my Nazi poet says, that 'the Creator placed life above law.' On the heels of this came the necessity to replace the idea of one's fellow man with a narrower idea, the idea of the proletariat or the Aryan, and instead of 'do no harm to your fellow man' they began saying 'do no harm to your country-man' or 'do no harm to a worker.' And now, my dear friend, I shall share with you my greatest doubt. Without religious and metaphysical underpinning, the word *man* is too ambiguous a term, is it not? From the moment it is deprived of traits such as an immortal soul and redemption through Christ, does it not disintegrate into a vast number of possibilities, of which some are better, others worse, some deserving of protection and cultivation, and others of absolute extinction? Finally, is it really possible to invent a single ethics, since the *daimonion*, left to its own resources, turns out to be something like Pythia? His pronouncements can be interpreted any which way, however one wishes – Mr Goebbels is well aware of this. I am not comforted in the least by the opinions of writers like Huxley. Rolling down a steep slope toward valleys inhabited by the wolves of totalitarianism, along with all of Europe, they seem to be unaware of this, and they mistake a brief period of as yet incompletely disrupted equilibrium between freedom and slavery for a permanent state. I am not comforted by allusions to European tradition; Europe's cart has driven more than once along this rutted path, but she has forgotten the dark moments of the past . . .

And so, what remains is to give up the attempt to discover an ethical authority in man, to shrug one's shoulders in response to the hopelessness of human justifications, and if one is to fight, then to do so only as a member of a threatened nation, only as enemy against enemy! There is something within me that rebels, something that demands that I assess justice and pass judgment on them both, the persecutor and the persecuted, according to a standard different from that of patriotic exaltation.

Allow me to end my letter with this doubt. May it balance out my frequent impulsiveness.

Speaking of a Mammal

I

Ten years ago, the news of Hiroshima found me in Cracow, and if I did not give it then the attention it deserved, it was because I was busy with something else. Anxious to preserve in a concrete form the vision of things newly seen, I was working on a scenario for a film. Its main figure was to be a city which before the war numbered more than a million inhabitants, but which, by the use of ordinary bombs and dynamite, was changed into a desert of burnt-out streets, twisted iron and crumbling barricades: this city was Warsaw. The idea of the film came to me from the story of a man who, after having lost his ties with civilization, had to face the world alone – Daniel Defoe's Robinson Crusoe. Once the Nazis had deported all the population which survived the battles of the Polish uprising of 1944, only isolated men, leading the lives of hunted animals, hid in the ruins of Warsaw. For every one of those men, the previous history of mankind had ceased to exist. They each had to solve anew the exceedingly difficult problem of finding water and crusts of bread in abandoned cellars; they were afraid to light a fire lest they betray their presence; and they trembled at the echo of a human voice.

My intention was to portray a Robinson Crusoe of our times. The earlier Crusoe's misfortune was to find himself on a scrap of land not yet touched by the power of mind capable of transforming matter. The misfortune of my Crusoe came about as a result of the use of the power of mind over matter for suicidal aims.

A few years later the film was produced by the State-owned Polish Film Company. Before shooting, however, the scenario provoked so many serious political objections that the producers had to make constant revisions every few months – without my participation. For Robinson Crusoe is, as we know, an asocial individual. His faithful Friday does not suffice to create a society. So the producers introduced two Fridays, and then again two, until the number reached a dozen, all imbued with a fine ideological zeal. They even included a heroic Soviet parachutist (yet unknown at that period in Warsaw). Thus, a film whose original purpose was to show the terrible landscape of a dead city and to warn men of their folly was transformed into a piece of paltry propaganda. Not only was it a deformation of truth; it was completely counter to truth.

I have recounted this adventure in order to draw from it a number of conclusions. That summer of 1945, when the blast over Hiroshima revealed the omnipotence of Faust, who started his career around 1505 by delving in magic, I was walking along the medieval streets of Cracow trying to push my political passions to the side. I had all the reason in the world to hate the Nazis, but to show that hatred in the film would have diminished the force of evil of which they were only an instrument. Rather, I preferred simply to mark their presence as a lurking danger. Without any sympathy for Stalin and Beria, I passed over their part in the destruction of Warsaw also. The important thing was the ruins, and the man who lived in them, an average man, a worker in his forties who never studied magic or social doctrines, whose problem was to survive in a city which our civilization had created and then transformed into a desert.

The conflict between that concept and the wishes of the Polish film directors was serious and in a sense symbolic. That the directors represented the

Communist Party, and that they tried to use the film to the immediate advantage of the Party, was only one facet of the problem. In trying to avoid 'deviation' they committed an absurdity: their attitude serves to point up the incommensurability between Faust's technical progress and his knowledge about himself. 'What is man?' I wanted to ask. 'Let us not stop at such a vague notion!' they exclaimed. 'What we want to know is whether he is a friend or an enemy. How can we tell if in your film he appears alone?' 'He is a victim,' I replied.

2

For many centuries, no one questioned the existence of 'human nature.' It was protected by the authority of the religions which erected a barrier between man and the rest of creation; a justified barrier, since no animal has a consciousness of time, nor does it know that it has to die. In order that a mentality such as that of the Polish film directors could arise (for me they are an example of politics in the pure state), it was first necessary that there be a steady development of scientific research and that this development be linked to the movement of historical transformations. At first, the earth ceased to be the center of the universe;

then the evolution of organisms became universally accepted; and as the human fetus was shown to repeat at certain stages in its development aspects of the life cycles of other species – to possess in fact some of the features of fish and frog – it was denied that human beings could pretend to be different from other living matter.

The promulgators of the nineteenth century's social doctrines were, however, torn between conflicting motives: between their quest to subject all phenomena to scientific law and their insistence on engineered social change. On the one hand, they leaned heavily upon biology where it helped them to abolish *ius naturale* and to supplant the concept of the immutability of moral rules with that of continuous change. But at the same time, they revolted against those biological tenets which held that man was subject to the same primitive struggle for life which characterizes the lower species. If what is called 'instinct' were always man's guiding inspiration, he would merely be a part of nature, and the hope of constructing an ideal society would prove illusory. Hence the fierce anti-naturalism of the Marxists, finding expression in their revulsion at a literature which portrayed the most elementary forces of sex and of violence. They are even more hostile to the idea of a special divine privilege, thanks to which man would carry within himself a set of inextricable aspirations and limitations. Seeking a specific difference between man and other vertebrates, Marxists found it in the fact that no animal has a history as the sum of transmittable experiences. To try to speak of man outside his historical context is to speak or a leaf without a tree. It is clear therefore why they interpret Defoe's Robinson Crusoe as only a tale about a young English merchant of the seventeenth century who treats his island as a capitalistic enterprise and so carries Society within himself – and why my Robinson Crusoe caused them lively anxiety.

The Marxist dilemma only symbolizes the confusion that has arisen over our concept of man: deprived by scientific critique of its root in metaphysics, humanitarianism has become either shallow or ineffective. The mechanistic notion of the universe which was the basis of science simply did not square with the notion of individual choice which is the basis of moral philosophy, Since my early youth – and I have lived in a time not particularly favorable for Europe – I have heard bitter words directed at humanitarians who clasp their hands piously in sorrow over cruelty yet are incapable of proposing means to combat it. I am familiar with a great number of literary works whose subject is the defeat of defenseless goodness; the heart bursting with eagerness to help fellow creatures regardless of their race, religion, or political affiliations is scorned by authors whose sarcasm hides their betrayed love. And it must be conceded that the position of humanitarianism is very weak. If the Vatican refers to the dignity of man, it does so in accordance with logic, for it backs it with metaphysical essence; while the tenderhearted intellectuals are the inheritors of a scientific view of life, and the concern they show for the intelligent animal among whose total achievements can be found such items as slavery, concentration camps, and gas chambers does not seem sufficiently motivated. As they have been unable to found any value through science, they have taken recourse in half-measures: they either do not confess that they are metaphysicians, or they are imperfect, half-hearted Marxists who deserve a condescending smile from the true Marxists for not taking the only step which could lead them, in any case apparently, out of the impasse: namely, to 'engage' themselves in history and politics. Yet if the 'humanitarians' did submerge themselves in history, they would be forced to renounce a *general* sympathy for all, and simply wish life to friends and death to enemies.

It is enough to establish the weakness of their basic premise; we must avoid proposing remedies which would be easy but ineffective. An element of pathos has been introduced by the fact that the eminent Western scientists who foresaw the danger from the use of atomic energy belong to that humanitarian type. With concern for all the inhabitants of our planet, they advance the opinion that an atomic war would bring extinction to all mankind, and this reflects their groping for a common denominator which would enable us to grasp the substance of man and thus recreate a feeling of planetary community. But their efforts often have to start from zero because of a too-complete insertion of the human species into the chain of evolution forged in the nineteenth century. The British biologist Haldane exclaimed at an international congress, 'I am proud that I am a mammal!'

The greatness and the defeat of the humanitarians are reflected in the figure of Albert Einstein. Many things were changed by his death; his former adversaries today pretend to have been his admirers. In Warsaw, when the reconstructed city is decked out for the numerous congresses and festivals, huge portraits of Newton and Einstein are hung on the fronts of the houses in the neighborhood of Copernicus' monument. It was not so during Einstein's lifetime. The Theory of Relativity, however much it was discussed in small specialist circles, was considered bourgeois and hence was not mentioned in public.

His warnings about the catastrophic possibilities of atomic power were received with the prescribed shrugs of the shoulder.

'The World Movement for the Defense of Peace' came into being through the initiative of a few Polish Communists, and the first Congress for the Defense of Peace took place in Poland, in 1948, in, Wrocław. On that occasion Einstein sent a message which raised panic among the organizers. He had displayed the extraordinary lack of tact to speak in it in the defense of all mankind, leaving no possibility for a division into bad men and good men, i.e., for demonology, which was after all what really mattered. He proposed as the only successful means of salvation the creation of a world government capable of controlling atomic energy. The message itself was not read. In order not to lose an important propaganda effect, however, a falsification was committed: a short letter which Einstein had enclosed with his message was presented as the message. These facts can be easily verified; the *New York Times* published the two texts, together with a short commentary by Einstein.

The same reasons that led the successor to Newton to be considered in the East as a harmless crank exposed him in America to the reproach of naiveté. His sense of responsibility as, the father of the Bomb forced him to condemn a lack of foresight in the United States similar to that of the participants at the Wrocław Congress. In so doing, he brought upon himself the suspicion of softness and almost of sympathy with the Reds. To his eternal glory it should be said that he tried until the very end to awaken world public opinion – in this twentieth century lacking a unifying principle. The last appeal – that of Bertrand Russell – which he signed does not deny the existence of a 'titanic struggle between Communism and anti-Communism,' but asks us to consider ourselves above all as 'members of a biological species which has had a remarkable history, and whose disappearance none of us can desire.'

One wonders whether this minimum definition 'biological species' can serve as a bridge connecting believers in mutually hostile philosophies. The nudity of that definition, after the thousands of years of creative thought which produced works of art, subtle constructions of dogma and meditations upon the qualities of the soul, is depressing. In any case, it shows the seriousness of the present moment. No prisoner of a concentration camp of our era would dream of asking pity for himself in the name of biological kinship with those who condemned him; he knows that he was discarded by them as historically harmful, and it is that harmfulness which defines him in the first place, and not his membership in the tribe of *Homo sapiens*. Cosmic perspective has been completely lost, and the best image of the earth would be of a ship on which the passengers murder each other, indifferent to the sea surrounding them. For politicians brought up on Leninist-Stalinist strategy, the acquisition of the new perspective called for in the last appeal signed by Einstein will be very difficult. Training inclines them to see in every call to hold fast to the helm either a ruse or a sign of resignation from the use of one's arms, an indication of a lack of faith in one's own forces. Yet they cannot fail to see something revolutionary in the enforced moral discipline: the humanitarians clearly and for the first time since the nineteenth century are realists as well. In the West, if people are moved by that appeal, it is by the very nudity of the term used. The scientists who wished to reach out to all mankind eventually concluded that it was hopeless to continue to refer to fraternity, to the special vocation of man, to human rights – and by this withdrawal, they relegated those words to a dying phraseology. We are confronted, thus, by a crucial manifesto which concedes that we do not possess any universally accepted language to express 'the quality of being man.'

3

If I permitted myself to start this article with a picture of Warsaw destroyed, it was not without the intention of showing how different the mental climate in Europe was from that in America at the moment when the newspapers brought the announcement of the greatest discovery ever made. The 'acceleration of history' in the few decades preceding that discovery was sensed by the Americans only as continuous technical progress, and the act of liberating atomic energy appeared to their eyes as something nearly divine, as well as demoniac and tragic; it was a sudden shock. In Europe, this 'acceleration of history' demonstrated its force in the span of one generation: the First World War broke out; seemingly indestructible powers – the Russian Czarist Empire and the Habsburg monarchy – fell; the Revolution of 1917 flared up; Nazism and Fascism culminated in the Second World War and Russia marched far beyond its 1914 borders, taking into its orbit little countries which had previously separated themselves from it, as well as nearly all the former Habsburg domain. To one witnessing these events, the rise and decline of State organisms, the appearance and disappearance of chiefs, the millions of graves and the ashes of other millions scattered over the fields, all combined to make up a film running at a crazy tempo. Human affairs had exploded like the mushroom of the atomic blast. As for technical advancement, it turned to the witness its ominous face – nights of bombardment, electrified barbed wire around borders, factories producing soap made from human fat, trailer trucks transformed into portable gas chambers in which were being exterminated the 'mammals' that filled Haldane with such pride, while a driver executioner quietly smoked his pipe. Hiroshima did not introduce anything startling into that picture. On the contrary, it was received as something that was inevitable.

These violent events were accompanied by phenomena in the field of thought which can be compared to a chain reaction. We can assign to the nineteenth century the role of a scholar's study room in which concepts were elaborated that to the contemporaries of the period seemed but theoretical; although in the succeeding century these same concepts managed to move heaven and earth. To complete the analogy with the development of physics, all the doctrines that people have accepted as worthy of being enriched with their very blood were born in the same Germany that is the source of the Bomb. Hegel,

Feuerbach, Marx, and Nietzsche were Germans, and it is rightly being said that the common feature of their teachings is their portrayal of the stupefaction of man when he recognizes that beyond him there is nobody in the Universe, and that he does not owe his attributes to any deity. In the past, Faust made his pact with the Devil. In the nineteenth century he rejected that help as an infringement upon his independence. For Hegel, God dissolved into the Movement, identified Himself with the Movement. For Feuerbach, and after him Marx, He became a humiliating product of the 'alienation.' In the 'God is dead' of Nietzsche, there is as much of triumph as there is of pain. Yet not until the twentieth century were conditions created in which the awareness of the new situation could spread, and what had been Promethean upheavals would be looked upon as commonplace. European literature, concealing philosophy under a symbol and a parable, faithfully notes this awakening.

'How to create Value?' – this is the question continuously repeated in that literature. If all Value has its source only in man, and he himself genuflects before what he has made an object of worship, he must be tortured by doubt as to his choice of idol, because he evidently could have chosen something else. Some of the writers worshipped before the altar of Art as the most autonomous and self-sufficient activity. This did not satisfy those more passionate, those who were moralists by temperament. We can see for how long a period of time these problems continued to absorb the attention of writers when we look at a few dates. Let as remember that Kafka's *Trial* was written as early as 1914 – and that Kafka (who died in 1924) achieved fame in Europe in the thirties. The moralists wandered through the 'arid plain' of T. S. Eliot waiting for a new revelation; since it was not forthcoming, they proclaimed catastrophe. Very early, around 1913, some of them discovered a general panacea for all ailments: action, and from that time on, action (political) has been the main problem of European literature. This penchant can be explained by ascribing demiurgical qualities to the Act of Faust, not only as far as the shaping of matter is concerned: action creates Value, thus man becomes a god.

The first movement to proclaim this openly was futurism; its creator, Marinetti, later supported Mussolini. Yet it would not be correct – although it is often done – to link the cult of action for action's sake to the extreme Right or Fascist movements alone. The most eminent Communist writers in Europe used first to reach the outermost limits of nihilism, and then, if they did not commit suicide, ended by finding a haven of faith in the Revolution, using it, as we might suppose, as a drug without which life and creation would have been impossible for them. This was the path followed by Mayakovsky, son of a family of public officials, who started out by embracing futurism; by Bertholt Brecht, a nihilist ironist in his first phase; by the sophisticated French poets Aragon and Éluard; and by many others.

One of the most interesting cases of polarization is Malraux, an author typical of the period we are dealing with, who placed his faith in the autonomous grandeur of man, at first in revolution, then in the history of art. Here we should come to a halt – although it is difficult to resist a glance into the future, and to hold back comment on some of the new barrels for the old wine. It is the word 'engagement,' introduced after the Second World War, that now holds our attention, as well as the renaissance in France of German philosophy, particularly that of Hegel via Sartre.

If one wished to assemble an anthology of writing in the various European languages for the period of 1930 to 1939 in which the approaching annihilation was predicted with despair, fear, or sometimes even joy, he would find himself with a collection almost the size of an entire library. There is nothing strange in the fact that for a great number of Europeans experiencing the oppressive atmosphere of those years and the sufferings of war, there existed a connection between anticipation and accomplishment. Nazism liquidated what illusions remained about the innate goodness of man, and discouraged people from relying upon their irrational impulses. Alone in the universe – and unable to rely upon his own instincts – where was a prisoner, or a relative of a prisoner or of a man shot to death, to look for rescue? The successes of Communism among the intellectuals were due mainly to their desire to have Value guaranteed, if not by God, at least by history. With resistance, but at the same time with relief, they subjected themselves to a discipline which liberated them from themselves.

While in America atomic energy quickly became a main topic of conversations, articles, and books, and served to arouse the collective anxieties, nothing similar could be observed on the European continent. There apocalypse was routine. The great majority of the inhabitants of the countries which found themselves within the Russian orbit avidly awaited the dropping of bombs on the heads of their new masters, or even on their own. In Poland, unknown hands covered the walls of factories during the night with pleas to Truman to come to a decision. In the Western part of the continent, the possibility of a quick mass death was received as not the worst eventuality – and people returned to their everyday occupations. This culminating achievement of scientific technique was reached at the moment of Europe's political, economic, and spiritual defeat, when, having exported its anti-transcendentalist philosophy to Russia and its technique to America, it passively watched how its own rays, projected onto the crystals of foreign civilizations, were reflected back upon itself. Flightiness, or apathy, or rather the great weariness of people who have lost much, who do not make plans because their future does not depend on them, not only made it impossible for them to accept as a real possibility that the Promethean effort of Faust could well mean the end of the long career of the species; it also closed their eyes to the vistas opened up by the rational use of nuclear energy for the prosperity of the species.

In the nineteenth century, continental Europe produced a writer of genius in the field of science fiction: Jules Verne, whose writings were a testimonial to Europe's faith in continuous progress. Today, however, if the European public reads about heroes of the distant future, it finds them in translations from America. This does not mean that Europeans are insensitive to those visions; the dimension of time remains, after the disappearance of the dimension of eternity, the only sphere of hope. Perhaps with the beginning of interplanetary voyages, hope will find new nourishment in the dimension of space, as in the era of the explorations of the earth in the sixteenth, seventeenth, and eighteenth centuries. As to the public in the Popular Democracies, its vision of the future comes from different sources; it must live not in the sad present, but in expectation of the perfect future happiness of grandchildren and great-grandchildren – a much more enticing happiness than that offered by American science fiction. The only flaw one can find in this vision is that such perfection can only be attained after the 'final battle' for the earth has been fought. Speaking to his son, a poet of a Popular Democracy tells the boy that he will see during his own lifetime 'an immense rainbow erected across the sky'; and he compares history to a patient weaver who intertwines his threads in such a way that they eventually will form the most beautiful pattern attainable.

4

As a consequence of the foregoing circumstances, Einstein's warning, which urges humanity to acquire a completely new perspective, will not strike a responsive chord among those Western European intellectuals who are keeping themselves busy discussing the adventures of dialectics. Reading their books, it is impossible to resist feeling that they are trying to relive a philosophical pageant staged a hundred years ago in Germany – while in America and Russia the sequel is being actively performed. These intellectuals would prefer to suffer the greatest humiliations rather than concede that they are conservatives untouched by the potentialities of the Atomic Era. But the complexity and diversity of Europe are such that their work, together with the instinctive unwillingness of the masses to face the too-difficult dilemma, nevertheless accomplish a useful function through the interplay of these two elements with less conspicuous tendencies of thought. This useful function might be described as that of a brake on the desperate impulses of the modern mind to fall far back, beyond the evil which resulted from reaching for forbidden fruit from the tree of knowledge.

The 'tragic sense' awakened by the shock of the first blast turned a few Americans to a kind of religion which is a negation of human achievements. What is more natural, after all, in the final hour of accounting, than to condemn Faust's first pact with the Prince of Shame who offered him eternal youth? The long story of the presumption of Reason is said to have begun with the Renaissance; at the outermost limits, punishment was waiting. Is it not then only fair to recognize the error and to concede with humility that the disappearance of the very substance of man shows us the overly high price we paid for the progress of science?

The Europeans who, thanks to their experiences, domesticated, so to speak, the 'tragic sense' view such repentance with suspicion, finding in it a temptation to simplify what should not be simplified. Too-easy solutions can have a very harmful effect when we have to accomplish a task which requires patience. The centuries which separate us from the Middle Ages are not like a blackboard which can be easily sponged off, leaving no trace of what had previously been written on it; we can no longer accept as our own the view of life of Dante, while at the same time launching artificial satellites into the ionosphere. That static image of the world is inaccessible to us; it was not known at that time that man is a historical being and is submitted to society to such an extent that the very air he breathes is conditioned by it. The importance of Marxism, always in the foreground of European quarrels, is that it forbids us to forget that fact; but man cannot be reduced to just a part in history; history is unable to produce a moral judgment unless we ascribe magic qualities to it. Marx saw that history is subjected to determinism, that it is of the realm of matter. It is extraordinary therefore that in looking for *justice*, he ascribed to matter a capacity for producing justice. After all, why does history subjected to necessity automatically produce a happy Communist society? What god watches over it? We can understand that matter through evolution produced man. Why should it care that he be happy and live in a happy society? No one yet can understand why matter should have been 'a machine for the manufacture of Good,' as Simone Weil says. This is the main contradiction at the base of today's major philosophical controversy, and it cannot be bypassed.

Now, it would not be fair to leave the picture as I have painted it. Life in Europe, through all the great disasters which have fallen upon it in succession, would be impossible if it were not for the existence of some subterranean rivers that only once in a while reveal their presence. Access to them is difficult, and the initiated do not like to show others the paths leading to them; these are rivers of jealously guarded hope. In the Western part of the continent, as in the Popular Democracies, those who quench their thirst at these waters recognize each other instantly with the first words spoken. Occasionally one of these rivers comes to the surface, and we give it the name of a person. One such person is Simone Weil. Her very style distinguishes her writings from the sentimental works of the demagogues. We immediately recognize that her attention is concentrated on the central problem of recovering the notion of human nature. Yet her approach is wary, as is the way of all those who have no illusions about the possibility of returning to a point left behind long ago, and who appreciate the new instruments placed at our disposal. It is no accident that she is constantly concerned with the philosophical bases of Marxism, which she considers 'the highest spiritual expression of bourgeois society.' From a criticism of an internal contradiction in Marxism between its scientific element and its prophetic element, she comes to a criticism of all attitudes which attempt to overcome the contradiction inherent in man by masking it, and create in this manner an artificial unity.

'The essential contradiction in human life,' she says, 'is that man, having as his very being a striving toward the Good, at the same time is submitted in all his being, in his thought as well as in his body, to a blind force, to a necessity that is absolutely indifferent to the Good. This is the way things are; and this is why no human thinking can escape from the contradiction.'

We can deal with the contradiction in two ways: 'The illegitimate way is to put together incompatible thoughts as if they were compatible with each other. (For instance, matter as a machine for the manufacture of Good.) The legitimate way, in the first instance, when two incompatible thoughts come to mind, is to exhaust all the resources of one's intelligence to try to eliminate at least one of the two. If that is impossible, if both impose themselves, we must then recognize the contradiction as a fact. Then, we must use it as if it were a tool with two prongs, like a pair of pliers, to enable us to enter, with its help, into direct contact with the transcendent domain of the truth inaccessible to human faculties.'

It is worth mentioning that Weil finds the equivalent of that procedure in mathematics. Her thinking, like that of others moving in the same direction, does not counsel resignation; on the contrary, it seeks to recognize limitations and to profit from that 'limit situation.' Her writings hold an additional interest for me because there are many similarly inclined minds in the Popular Democracies. Since all youth there is given Marxist schooling, the intellectual movement is intense. Young people are put in touch with one of the most complicated of philosophies; they come out of it either with little more than a certain number of easily assimilated slogans, or else with a desire to pull down the wall of these slogans – and then they see for the first time the vicious circle of historically determined ethics. The frequent cases of conversion of young Marxists to Catholicism are but one of the symptoms. It happens more frequently than not, that dialectical materialism is being secretly considered as merely an efficient work theory, unable to provide answers to more basic questions.

I would not like to conclude this article by making too-far-reaching prognostications. Granting that Faust needs two poles, that of creation and that of destruction, it is difficult to believe that he would not someday be able to recover the equilibrium at present lost between them. This may take much time. Yet we would be unjust if, living in a period when destruction prevails, we were to accuse him of being only a criminal. Let us rather assume that he is now again entering the stage of research on man to which he is compelled by discoveries in physics. He has left this field fallow in the past, and he concedes it. Neither Hegel, nor Marx, nor Nietzsche provided him with the tools; or rather, they provided him with tools ill-adapted for the immense territory waiting for the plow. But Faust does make valiant attempts, again and again, with what is at his disposal. A certain European fatalism, which advises men to plant the apple trees today, even if the end of the world were to come tomorrow, can be of help to him; it counsels him to do, at all costs, what must be done – even though it is quite possible that death will overtake him in the act.

Essay in Which the Author Confesses That He Is On the Side of Man, for Lack of Anything Better

I have often been asked why I, a poet, with a clear-cut vocation, engage in inanities; that is, write about things which can be grasped only in an improvised fashion, resisting precision. I, too, reproach myself for this and am consoled by the fact that, thus far, I have not written panegyrics in honor of any contemporary statesman – although more than once I have expended time on projects perhaps no less useless. But what I am doing now is not without function, at least for me. I am examining what is hidden behind my tendency to slip into social themes.

The world, existence, may be conceived as a tragedy, but, unfortunately, that view is no longer our specialty. Tragedy is grave, hieratic, while today we are assailed at every moment by monstrous humor, grotesque crime, macabre virtue. The dismal antics in which we all, willingly or not, have taken part (for these antics were History with a capital *H*) seemed to enjoin us to sprinkle our heads with ashes and weep like Job – but our Job shook with laughter for his own fate and, at the same time, for the fate of others. Every television switched on, every newspaper taken in hand evokes pity and terror, but a derisive pity, a derisive terror. I am no exception: while sympathizing with the victims of terror, I cannot control the sarcastic spasms wrenching my face when, for example, I learn that the police of a certain totalitarian state have made a series of arrests disguised as doctors and hospital attendants, having also painted their police cars with red crosses to look like ambulances. Those arrested were beaten unconscious, then carried off on stretchers by the 'attendants.' As has already been observed many times, reality's nightmarish incongruence has outstripped the boldest fantasies of the satirists. The entire style of my century is an attempt to keep pace with this depressing and ridiculous abomination, and can be felt in drawings, paintings, theater, poetry, the style of the absurd, and in our fierce and bitter jeering at ourselves and the human condition.

This style unites everything: the solitude of man in the universe, his imagination disinherited from a space related to God; images of what is taking place on the surface of the entire planet, which are constantly bombarding us; the neo-Manichaean hatred for matter; Promethean defiance in the name of human suffering is sent into a void, since there is no addressee. This medley of ingredients makes for an ambivalent style, and nearly every work can be interpreted with equal validity either as metaphysical despair or as a curse hurled at man's cruelty to man, at evil society.

I do not like the style of the absurd and do not wish to pay it homage by using it, even if I am assured that it derives from protest. Black gallows humor is too much an admission of complete impotence; mockery has long been the only revenge for the humiliated, the oppressed, slaves. Although today's sensibility is so blunted that, without the stimulation of tricks from the Grand Guignol, our voice is heard by practically no one, contempt for fashion has, on the whole, kept me from making concessions. Possibly my need for order is exceptionally great, or perhaps I am classical in my tastes, or perhaps mine are the ways of a polite, naive boy who received a Catholic upbringing. I think, however, that in my need for order, my reluctance to grimace hellishly in response to the absurd, I am quite average, except that I am less ashamed of my heart's demands than other people.

I do not like the style of the absurd, but neither do I like the natural order, which means submission to blind necessity, to the force of gravity, all that which is opposed to meaning and thus offends my mind. As a creature of flesh, I am part of that order, but it is without my consent. And with absolute sobriety I maintain that although today our imagination cannot deal with a division of existence into the three zones of Heaven, Earth, and Hell, such a division is inevitable. Man is inwardly contradictory because he resides in between. For me, the talk of some Catholics – wishing to buy their way into the good graces of the unbelievers – about the goodness of the world, is no more than a fairy tale. On the contrary, I do agree with Simone Weil when she says that the Devil does not bear the title Prince of This world in vain. Certainly, the causes and effects that govern matter with mathematical necessity do not entitle us to hurl abuse at God or at any X designating the very basis of existence. If we can leave our humanity aside for a moment and put our human sense of values out of mind, we must admit that the world is neither good nor evil, that such categories do not apply to the life of a butterfly or a crab. It is, however, another matter when we are dealing with our own demands, demands peculiar to us amid everything alive. Then indifferent determinism assumes diabolical features and we have the right to suppose that God has leased the universe to the devil, who, in the book of Job, is one of Jehovah's sons. 'The war we wage with the world, the flesh, and the Devil' is not a contrivance of Spanish mystics but occurs within us and as well between us and the indifferent necessity surrounding us. I am twofold: to the degree that I am the kin of the butterfly and the crab, I am the servant of the Spirit of the Earth, who is not good. If there were no man, there would be no Devil, for the natural order would not have been contradicted by anyone. Since it is contradicted, its ruler, Satan, the Spirit of the Earth, the demiurge of nature, battles with what is divine in man for the human soul. And only the covenant with God allows man to disengage himself, or rather to attempt to disengage himself, from the net of immutable laws binding creation.

I am, thus, frankly pessimistic in appraising life, for it is chiefly composed of pain and the fear of death, and it seems to me that a man who has succeeded in living a day without physical suffering should consider himself perfectly happy. The Prince of This World is also the Prince of Lies and the Prince of Darkness. The old Iranian myths about the struggle of Darkness with Light, Ahriman against Ormazd, suit me perfectly. What, then, is the light? The divine in man turning against the natural in him – in other words, intelligence dissenting from 'meaning-lessness,' searching for meaning, grafted onto darkness like a noble shoot onto a wild tree, growing greater and stronger only in and through man.

Consciousness, intelligence, light, grace, the love of the good – such subtle distinctions are not my concern; for me it is enough that we have some faculty that makes us alien, intruders in the world, solitary creatures unable to communicate with crabs, birds, animals. According to an old legend common in the first centuries of Christianity and later forgotten, Satan revolted because God ordered him, the firstborn, to pay homage to man, who had been created in God's likeness and image. From then on, all Satan's activities have had a single aim – to rival the younger brother so unjustly exalted. Or, to offer a somewhat different reading, enmity was established between us and nature.

We are unable to live nakedly. We must constantly wrap ourselves in a cocoon of mental constructs, our changing styles of philosophy, poetry, art. We invest meaning in that which is opposed to meaning; that ceaseless labor, that spinning is the most purely human of our activities. For the threads spun by our ancestors do not perish, they are preserved; we alone among living creatures have a history, we move in a gigantic labyrinth where the present and the past are interwoven. That labyrinth protects and consoles us, for it is anti-nature. Death is a humiliation because it tears us away from words, the sounds of music, configurations of line and color, away from all the manifestations of our anti-natural freedom, and puts us under the sway of necessity, relegates us to the kingdom of inertia, senseless birth, and senseless decay.

Yes, but the absurdity that afflicts us today is, first and foremost, the work of man. Civilization does not satisfy our desire for order, for clear, transparent structure, for justice, and finally, for what we instinctively apprehend as the fitness of things. The savagery of the struggle for existence is not averted in civilization. Opaque, automatic, subordinate to the most primitive determinants, and subordinating us so much that it levels and grinds us down, civilization does not approach but rather recedes from the models of a republic at long last fit for man, as postulated by philosophers for more than two millennia. That happens because the duality residing in each of us is in fact sharpened by civilization. The Devil brilliantly exploits technology in order to penetrate to the interior of our fortress and manipulate our mechanisms; that is, the determinism and inertia of what is not human drags what is divine in man down as well.

For many of my contemporaries, the Devil is the inventive, coldly logical mind, as well as the creator of the technological civilization by which we are increasingly elevated and oppressed. For that reason, many people side with the instincts and intuition of natural, individual man against the artificial and the collective. It is also true that in the popular imagination the self-confident know-it-all with his books, reducing everything to the mechanisms of cause and effect – dry, devoid of faith, indifferent to good and evil – has often been synonymous with the evil spirit. This image is maintained by the comics, film, and television, where the villain, a criminal in a white lab coat, is made omnipotent by his laboratory. For me, however, the responsibility for our misfortunes is not borne by intellect but by intellect unenlightened, insufficiently rational, cutting itself off from those gifts of ours – grace or attachment to value, by whatever name – from which it should be inseparable. I am no friend of the rationalists either those of the eighteenth century or their successors. But if today's opponents of impersonal, repressive, inhuman knowledge are quick to cite William Blake, I am with them only because I find in Blake something different than they do. The intellect that oppressed Blake renounced impulse in favor of the fixed laws of matter, and renounced ascending movement in favor of inertia. Newton's physics horrified Blake because he saw them as a declaration of subjection, our subjection to what is; since things are as they are, there is no choice in the matter.

In modern times the great metaphysical operation has been the attempt to invest history with meaning. That is, we, as foreigners, intruders, face a world that knows neither good nor evil; our divinity is weak, imprisoned in flesh, subject to time and death; so let our labyrinth but increase, let our law, born of the challenge we hurl at the world in the name of what should be, be established. Our existence, like that of crabs and butterflies, does not lend itself to deliberations on its own purpose, all our *what fors* and *whys* fall away; meaning can only be made from what resists meaning if, from one generation to the next, there is an increase in the purely human need for justice and order, which also permits us to postulate the moment when humanity will be fulfilled. Curious dislocations and substitutions have occurred in the course of that attempt. God changed into a malevolent, cruel demiurge, the tyrant Zeus, the tyrant Jehovah, because he was the god of nature, which contradicts and dissatisfies us; many people have opposed that god with a divine hero, a leader of men, namely, the rebel Prometheus, Lucifer (who often had the face of Christ), as did the Romantic poets. Later, anyone who wished to see history in motion and directed toward a goal was required to express himself in the language of atheism. However, the change did not relieve this process of any of the traditional violence that occurs whenever ultimate concerns are at stake.

This much should be said lest I be suspected of possessing the instincts of an activist, which are, in fact, rather weak in me. The social and the political are forced onto us, since we have no defense against time and destruction outside of them. The labyrinth spun by the generations is so truly splendid, so interesting, that just to wander through it affords one much joy, and I do not blame people for never poking their noses from books or museums. And there is also the making of art, which is continually infusing human freedom with new life. But, upon closer examination, one sees that that entire humanistic space withers and dies if it's not stimulated by a reaching out from stagnant to new forms; while, by virtue of laws, which I shall not mention here, the new always allies itself with the social and the political, though sometimes in a highly roundabout way.

Our age has been justly called the age of new religious wars. That would make no sense if the Communist revolutions were not rooted in metaphysics; that is, had not been attempts to invest history with meaning through action. The liberation of man from subjection to the market is nothing but his liberation from the power of nature, because the market is an extension of the struggle for existence and nature's cruelty, in human society. The slogans used by the two camps, the adherents of the market and the revolutionaries, thus take on an aspect that is quite the reverse of what they seem at first sight. The enemies of revolution loved to appear as the defenders of a religion threatened by atheists while those atheists hated them as the priests of an inferior god, Zeus, Jehovah, otherwise known as the Devil, who tramples the divine impulses in man. This is the meaning of History which Marxism opposed to Nature. Marxism is thus in harmony with the neo Manichaean ferocity of modern man. Were it not, it would not exercise the near-magical attraction it has for the most active minds and would not be a central concern for philosophers.

Only when a metaphysical core is recognized in what seems to be merely social and political can the dimensions of the catastrophe that has befallen us be assessed. Hopeful thought moved into action and returned to thought, but now bereft of hope. The collapse of faith in the meaning of history as a result of the revolution which was both victorious and a failure concerns, to be sure, only Europe and North America, but we must have the nerve to admit that we neither can nor very much desire to share the hopes of Asians, Africans, and Latin Americans, for we assume tacitly, and perhaps quite wrongly, that there will be a repetition of a pattern with which we are already familiar.

It is easy to miss the essence of revolutionary intention, for it is usually obscured by sentimental and moralistic slogans. It is also easy to argue that what happened had to have happened. Marxism wanted to act against the Devil but let him in through a loophole in doctrine. That is, because of its scientific ambitions, Marxism glorified necessity, which supposedly was to be the midwife of men's freedom. In this manner, terror acquired the sanction of a *Weltgeist* invested with all the trappings of an evil demiurge. This was none too friendly a blessing for any better tomorrow. And thus, in the countries ruled by Marxists, the Prince of Lies put on a performance that made all his previous exploits pale by comparison. However, it should not be forgotten that, in retrospect, we are always inclined to ascribe to events more developmental logic than they in fact possessed.

What is the trap we are caught in today? My childhood was marked by two sets of events whose significance I see as more than social or political. One was the revolution in Russia, with all its various consequences. The other was the omen of Americanization, the films of Buster Keaton and Mary Pickford, the Ford motorcar. Now there is no doubt that Americanization has carried off complete victory: Americanization means the product of forces not only lower than man and not only outstripping him, submerging him, but, what is more important, sensed by man as both lower than and outstripping his will. Who knows, perhaps this is a punishment for man's claims on the forbidden. The more God abandoned space, the stronger became the dream of building the Kingdom of God here and now with our own hands, which, however, condemned man to a life of getting and spending. Fine, why should it be any other way? The only question is whether our twofold nature can endure a static reality, and whether we, if forbidden to reach out beyond that reality and beyond our nature, will not go mad, or, to use the language of psychiatrists, succumb to an excess of 'problems.' It may well be that we are healthy only when trying to leap from our own skins, in the hope of succeeding from time to time.

Something important, at least to me, emerges from what I have said. There seems to be much truth in what I have read in histories of religion about the circle symbolizing Greek thought. A circle has neither beginning nor end, on its circumference 'was' flows into 'is' and returns to 'was.' The exact opposite holds for Jewish thought, which is well depicted by the sign of the arrow. The flight of that arrow: the Covenant with God, the journey of the chosen people through the ages, the promise of a Messiah. This was inherited by Christianity, and it is the source of secular messianic dreams as well. Even the prosaic bourgeois concept of progress in the second half of the nineteenth century occasioned expectations that seem comical to us today, as can be seen in Bolesław Prus's novel *The Doll*, where the invention of a metal lighter than air was to assure universal peace and universal happiness. For me these are very personal matters. The education I received set me forever under the sign of the arrow, an education not confined to school. Yet in America, where I live, in this phase of civilization, every man must somehow cope with his situation – that of a fly trapped in amber. He is surrounded by that which has lost its ability to maintain direction and has begun to take on a circular form. Interplanetary voyages hold little promise of our entering another human dimension, and probably only the legend of flying saucers provides any outlet for our yearning for something completely other, through contact with little green men arriving here from some distant planet. The mind either behaves perversely, delighting in visions of destruction, catastrophe, apocalypse (in this respect, American intellectuals are reminiscent of their European colleagues of the twenties and thirties), or consoles itself with an eternally recurrent cosmic harmony in disharmony. Perhaps the circle is not an exact representation of Greek thought on time-space, but some kinship between Greece and India, and the present interest in Oriental wisdom may be a result of the restraints imposed upon our images of ascending movement.

In any case, America, by virtue of its entire development, whose driving force was automatic, unplanned movement, has always suffered from a certain weakness in historical imagination – yesterday and tomorrow are like today, a little worse, a little better, which is perhaps why in American films both ancient Romans and astronauts from the year 3000 look and act like boys from Kentucky. The imagination had a naturalistic orientation – man, eternally the same, eternally in the power of the same drives and needs, faced a nature also eternally the same. Commercial advertising fell into this pattern easily and contributed to its reinforcement. Advertising appeals to the physiological sides of what is 'eternally human': sex; the ingestion of food (appetizing dishes which make your mouth water); excretion (pills regulating the stomach, toilet paper delightful to the touch); ugly odors (mouthwashes, deodorants).

I am ill-disposed to the philosophical propositions that current literature, art, and advertising offer me. Every man and woman I pass on the street feels trapped by the boundaries of their skin, but, in fact, they are delicate receiving instruments whose spirituality and corporality vibrate in one specific manner because they have been set at one specific pitch. Each of them bears within himself a multitude of souls and, I maintain, of bodies as well, but only one soul and one body are at their disposal, the others remaining unliberated. By changing civilizations, time continually liberates new souls and bodies in man, and thus time is not a serpent devouring its own tail, though ordinary men and women do not know this. Once, a very long time ago, walking down the street in a Polish village, I grew thoughtful at the sight of ducks splashing about in a miserable puddle. I was struck because nearby there was a lovely stream flowing through an alder wood. 'Why don't they go over to the stream?' I asked an old peasant sitting on a bench in front of his hut. He answered: 'Bah, if only they knew!'

Saligia

Superbia
Avaritia
Luxuria
Invidia
Gula
Ira
Acedia

In the Middle Ages the first letters of the seven cardinal sins formed the word *saligia*, which was thought to be doubly useful since it made it easy to memorize the names of the seven sins, or, rather, failings (*vitia capitalia*),and it emphasized their unity. That much I knew, but not long ago I was tempted to look into a few encyclopedias to check out what they had to say about *saligia*. In none of them did I find even a mention of this word. What is more, Catholic encyclopedias and dictionaries of theological terms are silent about it. Priests no longer evince much interest in sins, as if they would like to ask the world's pardon for considering this one of their primary tasks for so many centuries. They mumble even when speaking of the concept of sin, and so they are not inclined to mention the old classifications in the compendia and catechisms that they edit.

In search of a certain book that is devoted to the history of the cardinal sins, I made my way to Theology Hill. For Berkeley, in addition to its university, which is splendid in every respect, also has several graduate divinity schools, for various denominations, which are located in close proximity to each other, with a lovely view of San Francisco Bay. They collaborate in an ecumenical spirit and share their rich library collections. The best known of these schools is the interdenominational Pacific School of Religion. The late Earl Morse Wilbur was a member of its faculty; he learned Polish in order to write his two-volume *History of Unitarianism*, not without a reason, for at least half his work is filled with the travels and disputes of the Polish Arians.

I found the book about the cardinal sins, but it was in storage, where rarely requested books are kept, which leads me to the conclusion that this topic is not particularly popular with either future pastors or their teachers. In fact, the list of cardinal sins compiled by the eremites of Egypt in the fourth century was always a bit of a historical relic, since the names of the sins would stay the same but their meanings kept changing. I learned from this work that the word *saligia* was popularized by Henry of Ostia in the thirteenth century, but that for a long time it was rivaled by another version: *siiaagl* (*superbia, invidia, ira, acedia, avaritia, gula, luxuria*), signifying a different ordering of the same failings. However, *saligia* triumphed, if only for mnemonic reasons, and was adopted by the Jesuits during the Counter-Reformation.

As a child, I did not receive much moral benefit from my catechism lessons. Perhaps children in general are not prepared to understand such convoluted knowledge, and besides, too many strange associations based on the Polish names for the cardinal sins would enter my mind during those lessons.

1. *Pycha* (pride) instead of *superbia*. *Pych* (punt), *puch* (fluff), *pyza* (a moon face or a round plate)? *Pyszałkowaty-pyzaty* (conceited and chubby)? Self-inflation beyond one's means? That's someone else, some gentleman, a *pyza-pycha w kryzie* (moon-faced, preening person wearing a ruff), definitely not I – in other words, this cannot apply to me. *Pycha* is classified instantly, just by its sound, whereas *superbia*, as Lucifer's attribute, has nuances of gravity, too, like English *pride*, French *orgueil*, German *Stolz*, Church Slavic *gordost'*.

2. *Łakomstwo* (covetousness) for *avaritia*. I saw in this a transgression that consisted of licking out jam jars or indulging my unrestrained craving for dessert, which may not be much of a problem today, but during my childhood desserts rarely appeared on our table. And who would have explained to me then that just such a yen for sweets was the mainspring of our civilization's grim history, that it provided the impetus for usury and the establishment of factories, for the conquest of America, the oppression of the peasant in Poland, the brilliant idea perfected by the pious citizens of Amsterdam that they could use their ships to traffic in slaves? Certainly, the mighty of this world have always wanted dessert. However, if they were at least gluttons, that is, individuals in pursuit of sensual pleasures, that wouldn't have been so bad. *Avaritia*, however, is rather an ascetic passion, as the French *avarice* and the German *Geiz* indicate. Should Molière's *L'Avare* be translated as *The Glutton*? English *covetousness* is closer to greediness than miserliness, but it is also a stern appetite directed exclusively at money. Both meanings, miserliness and greediness, are expressed by Church Slavic *srebrolub'e*, a literal translation of the Greek *filarguria*.

3. *Nieczystość* (impurity) instead of *luxuria*. This probably had something to do with not washing oneself? With the added implication of 'shameful

parts'? But the Latin word meant exuberance, fertility, abundance, primarily of vegetation, then immoderate exuberance, for example in how one expressed oneself; also excess, overweening pride, and dissolution. French *luxure* preserved some of these connotations, although it means the same as Polish *rozwiązłość* (dissoluteness); *rozwiązłość*, not *nieczystość*, would have been a better Polish equivalent. By abandoning Latin here and making use of the Old German *Lust*, English has strayed too far from the original meaning, although the adjective *lusty* leans in the direction of exuberant, strong, and at one time was used in the sense of playful, merry. English *lust* suggests the kind of changes that related concepts have been subjected to as a result of language and customs, especially if we compare it to the Church Slavic name for this sin: *blud* (which simply means 'fornication'), taken directly from Greek *porneia*, bypassing the Latin. *Nieczystość*, by contrast, appears to be simply a translation of the German *Unkeuschheit*.

4. *Zazdrość* (envy) instead of *invidia*. The meaning of this word was completely unclear to me. Now, I know that its souce is the Latin *in-videre*; *za-źrzeć*, in other words, exactly the same thing as *za-widzieć* (*zavist'* in Church Slavic). Other languages place more or less emphasis on will, yearning, although I find it difficult to say if French *envie*, English *envy*, German

Neid adequately convey the sense of the Latin term that includes both hatred and slander.

5. *Obżarstwo* (gluttony) and *pijaństwo* (drunkenness) instead of *gula*. Originally, it meant throat in Latin; later, voraciousness and greediness, too. Gluttony and drunkenness suggested an image of laden tables, of potbellied men grunting and bellowing: obviously a grownup's sin. Only now do I wonder why Polish used two words to translate *gula*. In none of the languages I know does drunkenness figure among the cardinal sins. Church Slavic *chrevougod'e*, or belly-pleasing, was constructed on the model of the Greek *gastrimargia*; the closest thing in Polish would have been *popuszozanie sobie pasa* (loosening one's belt) in relation to both food and drink. Something unexpected happened to this failing in the course of history, perhaps because there was a time in the past when more people could indulge themselves with *gula* than in the course of the following centuries. All sorts of undernourished people could lick their chops at the thought of stuffing their bellies just for once, and an entire poetry arose about smoked goose, kielbasa, smoked ham, kegs of beer. It was supposed to be a sin, but what else was the reward for self-restraint during Lent if not gluttony and drunkenness? And is there really a negative connotation to the French word *gourmandise*? On the contrary, if someone is a *gourmand* that's very good, it means he has a ruddy

complexion, ties his napkin under his chin, and is knowledgeable about cuisine and wines; he's not a pauper. He's not quite a *gourmet*, or a connoisseur of food, but he's close to it. German *unmässig* doesn't benefit from such privileges, and the English *glutton* is also different, an insatiable gullet prone to *gluttony* or omnivorousness.

6. *Gniew* (rage) instead of *ira*. 'An explosion of rage' – it wasn't hard to picture what that is. It is a short-lived physical state that is expressed in violent deeds (King Bolesław the Brave breaking into the church and in a fit of rage murdering the bishop). *Ira* doesn't present any great difficulty in translation either. *Anger, colère, Zorn*, Church Slavic *gnev*.

7. *Lenistwo* (laziness) instead of *acedia*. Polish is not responsible for the comical misunderstanding. The word is not Latin but was borrowed via the Latin directly from the Greek *akedia*, and should have been translated as *obojętność* (indifference). But for the fourth-century eremites *akedia* was the main danger, a temptation by the Devil that was most severe at noon, when all nature rests in silence, motionless under the high sun. That is when a monk would be visited by sadness and boredom. He would try to resist it with prayer, but he would be tormented by a feeling that all his exertions and his mortifications were meaning-less. If he allowed himself to be defeated, he would

abandon his cave and just run over to the neighboring cave in order not to be by himself. If he often succumbed to such attacks, he had to return to the city, to be among people. *Akedia* was therefore a dangerous impediment for people dedicated to an intense spiritual life. Monastic instructions also devoted a good deal of attention to it later on, in the Middle Ages. It was frequently linked with *tristitia* or *lupe*, that is, sadness; it is easiest to express it with the words *nothing matters*. The transformation of *akedia* into the (physical?) failing of somnolence and indolence took place only gradually. Neither the French *paresse*, the English *sloth*, nor the German *Trägheit* conveys the original meaning. Only Church Slavic *unyn'e* conveys it perfectly. Obviously, I didn't have the foggiest notion of what 'laziness' was except for one of its variants, that is, my understandable repugnance for 'iron necessity,' that is, doing my homework.

The disinclination of clergymen today to classify sins is understandable, since the whole great edifice of distinctions, concepts, and syllogisms was erected quite late, achieving its ultimate form in Jesuit casuistry. Of course, the prestige of scientific research that sets itself the task of dissecting stuffed bears in order to see how they are constructed undoubtedly also had an influence. This stuffed bear, or man, is not studied by psychologists as a tangle of good and evil, or of values, but as the territory of certain 'phenomena.' At the same time, man's poor sins, in comparison with the luxuriant flora and fauna discovered inside him, have become abstractions similar to émigré governments and exiled monarchs.

Nonetheless, *Sed contra*, as Thomas Aquinas used to say. In each of us various interesting chains of causes and effects can be tracked down, but let someone else concern himself with this. When we are alone with ourselves, it is our goodness and our evil that perturb us and not those intriguing questions: Where do we come from and why are we here? And what if I should try to ascertain what the cardinal sins, so vague and foggy in my childhood, mean to me today? This would be no ordinary assignment, because it would imply that a new content is being interpreted in terms of the old *saligia*; that is, by discovering its imposing forms within oneself, one restores it to its sorrowful dignity.

Let us be candid. The seven cardinal sins were considered at most a spur to the actions that condemn one to eternal damnation, but not a single one of these seven nor *saligia* as a whole had of necessity to lead to utter damnation. For the *vitia capitalia* were the more or less universal manifestations of spoiled human nature, and this nature is not so spoiled as to leave no room for hope. Thus, in *The Divine Comedy*, when Dante and his guide,

Virgil, emerge at the other end of the earth after their sojourn in Hell at the center of earth and begin their ascent to Mount Purgatory, they come upon seven terraces, each of which is inhabited by souls who are doing penance for one of the seven cardinal sins. The order of these terraces follows the model of *siiaagl*, not *saligia*, and I find Dante's reasoning convincing. Several tercets from Canto 17 are of particular importance here and are well worth citing in translation. When they reach the fourth terrace Virgil says:

> '*My son, there's no Creator and no creature*
> *who ever was without love – natural*
> *or mental; and you know that,' he began.*
>
> '*The natural is always without error,*
> *but mental love may choose an evil object* [per malo obietto]
> *or err through too much or too little vigor.*
>
> *As long as it's directed toward the First Good*
> *and tends toward secondary goods with measure,*
> *it cannot be the cause of evil pleasure;*
>
> *but when it twists toward evil, or attends*
> *to good with more or less care than it should,*
> *those whom He made have worked against their Maker.*
>
> *From this you see that – of necessity –*
> *love is the seed in you of every virtue*
> *and of all acts deserving punishment.'*

[TRANSLATED BY ALLEN MANDELBAUM]

'Love that moves the sun and the stars' is, then, the core of all things and of each living being. In the order of nature (*amore naturale*) it does not submit to moral judgments. A stone released from the hand falls because that is what the law of gravity wants; an animal hunts another animal because that is what he is ordered to do by what has come to be called instinct. But love in the spiritual order, which is what distinguishes man and also angels (*amore d'animo*), can be mistaken. Its calling is to aspire to the first good, that is, to the source of great good, that is, to God (*primo ben diretto*). It is mistaken if it recognizes as its good something that conflicts with this chief end, and also if it itself is too strong or too weak. The seven terraces of Purgatory are an illustration of such errors. The three lowest signify depraved love; that is, love that aspired to a mistaken goal. The souls whom Dante and Virgil meet there are suffering because during their lifetimes the magnetic needle of their love (or Will) had turned toward themselves: *superbia, invidia, ira*. The fourth is the terrace of *acedia*, or insufficient, somnolent love, that love that was incapable of putting to proper use the time given to mortal man. The three highest terraces, the ones closest to the Earthly Paradise, which is located on the highest plateau of Mount Purgatory, are designated as the place of penance for souls whose love was

excessive, because *avaritia, gula*, and *luxuria* derive
from excess. This is rather enigmatic, because the
greedy, the gluttonous, and the dissolute come out
much better with their failings than do others. Their
powerful will to life appears to be centrifugal, not
centripetal; that is, it is directed toward the external
world, toward its annexation. It is oblivious, somehow,
of the annexer himself: for the greedy man or the
miser, money symbolically summarizes all the delights
of earth; roast meats rivet the attention of the glutton
because he does not, after all, think about his own
taste – taste resides in the roast; a beautiful girl charms
the ladykiller with a promise of something mysterious,
unrecognized. If this is so, if the centrifugal will to
life is the pursuit of existence as enchantment, by
transgressing a certain measure it can find satiety only
in *primo ben diretto*, that is, in God; but in that case,
since there is so much of it, it would lead to saintliness.
But saintliness is not easy, which is why these three
higher terraces exist. Which is to say, since love
directed outward, so to speak, toward things appre-
hended by the senses, is not an error, at worst its
excessive greediness would incline one to offer this
advice: Either be saintly or you will have to have less
of this love of yours. Dostoevsky follows Dante
faithfully in *The Brothers Karamazov; the avaritia, gula*,
and *luxuria* of both the elder Karamazov and Dmitri

pale in comparison with a truly severe defect: Ivan's *superbia*, with which Smerdyakov's *acedia* is in league.[*]

Superbia

If you are one of the thousand, shall we say, active poets of your time, you think about what will become of your works in a hundred or two hundred years. Either all your names will be listed only in footnotes to the intellectual history of the period, or one of you will rise above the fashions and collective customs, while the rest, although they had appeared to be individuals, will form a chorus obedient to its conductor, who will silence any voices that are too independent – independent, that is, of the epoch's style. That one poet is you, for you alone are right. But what does poetry have in common with being right? A whole lot. The arrangement of words implies choice, choice implies deliberation, and behind your words lurks a silent judgment about the many human matters that you have dealt with. If in your judgment (conscious, semiconscious, or unconscious) you are

[*]Sergei Gessen was the first to apply *saligia* to Dostoevsky His 1928 work, 'Tragedna dobra v "Brat'rakh Karamazovykh,"' is reprinted in the collection *O Dostoevskom. Stat't* (Providence: Brown University Press, 1966), pp 199–229.

right, you will break through the cocoon of generally accepted opinions in your epoch; the others, however, will become trapped in them. For not all reasons are equal and error enjoys the same privileges as truth for only a short time. Could it be, then, that absolute criteria exist for the creations of the imagination and language? Without a doubt. But how can that be? After all, one person likes one thing, another likes something else, *de gustibus non est disputandum*. And yet everything that can be numbered among the works of the human spirit submits to a strict hierarchy. Our opinions about contemporary works are unstable and tentative, because only time lays bare the true hierarchy under the veils and piles of gilded rubbish. Nonetheless, at the moment when you hold your pen and compose poetry, you are extraordinarily confident of your rightness – and also of the erroneous assumptions of all your rivals. But isn't there a fraternity of poets who are also very different but who respect each other? There are such fraternities. The triumph of your mastery, however, is contained in the act of writing itself, and you know very well that you trust only the voice of your own daimonion.

It cannot be ruled out that this is the way things have worked up till now because 'eternal glory' has gotten into the habit of crowning only a few greats. Considering that it is the *activity* (writing, painting, sculpture, etc.) that assumes prominence today and not the results, it is possible that the many millions of creative artists who are fleetingly famous will replace the few who are chosen. I was raised according to traditional beliefs, however, and therefore I am inclined to consider the sin of *superbia* an occupational disease. If we limited its meaning to overweening pride, we would ignore the rich ambiguity of its consequences, for pride and self-assurance are indispensable for the poet who wishes to achieve something and not retreat from his path.

I have held various opinions about poetry and literature in various phases of my life, so I might be making the mistake of reading into the past the views that I hold today. In the profession of 'writer' I now see a certain embarrassing buffoonery. When we read the diaries of various masters of the pen published nowadays, we are overcome with pity: they really considered themselves 'great.' How many of them worshipped dry rot, their own renown, which was supported by a couple of coffeehouses and a handful of press clippings? That's how it is now, but my not very friendly attitude toward my profession was formed a long time ago, I think, in my early youth. Already at that time poetry, not to speak of literature in general, was *too little*. Let us assume that you are, potentially, better than your rivals (which I did not doubt). So what? Among the blind a one-eyed man is king, and are you really going to take pride in that title? There is no question that I wanted to be a superb poet. But that did not seem to me to be sufficient. Had I aspired to the composition of a certain number of excellent poems, that would simply have been evidence of only mild *superbia*; however, I had enough *superbia* in me for it to carry me beyond any mere authorship.

I did not ascribe to myself any extraordinary abilities or talents except for one which I would be unable to define even now. It was a particular type of intelligence capable of perceiving associations between things that others did not perceive as connected. It was also a type of imagination that was particularly sensitive to customs and institutions. One way or another, I always heard this warning inside me: *This cannot last*. And if there was a certain unreality to everything that surrounded me, could works written in the midst of this unreality be real? Especially since this did not apply to Poland alone but also, although for somewhat different reasons, to all of Europe. Somewhere, Ortega y Gasset compares the artist who is born in an unfavorable era to a woodcutter with strong muscles and a sharp ax who finds himself in the desert. I wasn't familiar with this analogy at that time, in my youth; had I known it, my auto-irony would have been expressed in the following words: 'You've picked a fine time, with that strength of yours, since there isn't any wood.'

It was necessary to strive for that dimension where the fates of both reality as a whole and poetry were being decided. However, it wasn't reachable by words in those days. Furthermore, no one understood my poems or, perhaps more important, I believed that no one understood them, because I felt totally isolated, the more so as we drew closer to 1939. Today, I understand this as follows: Polish society has a very strong sense of the sacral, and this explains the specific fortunes of Poles in a century of advanced desacralization. What we are talking about here, however, is such an extreme appropriation of the sacral by one goddess – Polishness – that nothing else was good enough for her. The dimension that my eyes dimly perceived in the thirties did not belong to the general Polish dimension, so my place was among the 'outsiders,' because they were Jews or because they were Communists or Communist sympathizers. No matter where I turned, however, there was nowhere where I felt at home. A taste for 'ultimate things' gave direction to my entire life, although due to various geographical-psychological peculiarities the Polish-Catholic tonality has not been dominant in this religion of mine.

Was my imagination right, then, to warn me that

this could not last? Here I should draw a distinction. Grasping the 'black' sides of reality, my imagination facilitated my pessimistic diagnosis, but I should try to downplay the opinion, flattering though it is, that this was my prophetic poetic gift at work. Who knows if my rejection of life in general, punishing it for being *unreasonable*, was not even more important here? This unreason, in both individual, biological life and collective life alike, has various degrees of intensity, ranging from those that can be named (e.g., economic absurdities, unsuccessful political institutions, and so forth) to completely elusive ones, though they were always inconsistent with my need for total harmony. Thus, whether the overthrow of the existing order occurred or not, its downfall would always have seemed justified to me in advance.

My *superbia* demanded punishment, and at last it has incurred punishment. For now, in my mature years, when I open my mouth and listen to myself with the ears of those to whom I speak, what do I hear? Incomprehensible babbling, which should be counted as punishment. After repeated explosions of rage (after all, I wasn't asking for much) I had to accept this immuring of myself in loneliness as equitable and pedagogically beneficial to me. Someone who writes in Polish should not harbor illusions. If the Polish custom of respect for literature as the national shrine did not go hand in hand with utter disdain for matters of the spirit, the earth would be too beautiful a place for our sojourn here.

To be polite: I am barely lifting the curtain here, conscious of the many complications that I have overlooked, for I am obedient to the discipline of language. I am limiting myself to the twofold consequences – negative and positive – of *superbia*. Does it not frequently act as a substitute for morality? As when it forbids us certain actions because they are beneath our conception of ourselves as worthy only of the highest acts? And could someone who relies on willfulness alone really get by without *superbia*? Sooner or later loneliness drives us into crises that cannot be resolved other than by some rebirth, the shedding of the snakeskin, so that what has tormented us till now no longer concerns us. True, I prefer to believe that my *superbia* has played the role of midwife at these births but that, independent of it, more noble characters have also been at work.

Invidia

He has what I ought to have; I, not he, deserve it – there's a model of envy. Not that I would like to be him; quite the contrary: he is inferior to me and has been unjustly rewarded, and undoubtedly, because of his inferiority, he is unable to even appreciate it (I, as the superior one, would be able to). Envy, the daughter of pride, is so widespread a failing among literati and authors that it's funny. For instance, every piece of news about a distinction accorded to others evokes in them more or less well-concealed pangs of jealousy. It is true that it is difficult to determine the extent and intensity of envy within oneself, because it is adept at disguising itself. Coming from a provincial European backwater and emigrating three times, first to Warsaw, then to Paris, then to America (always with a marshal's baton in my knapsack?), I must have been cultivating plenty of envy within myself. Let's be fair; this was moderated, however, by an exceptional talent for idolizing, so that while sternly judging some (the many), I knelt humbly before the chosen, absolutely convinced of my own utter inferiority (though they were rarely 'writers').

Let us abandon the field of art and literature, however. My century should have been called the age of *invidia* and I shall explain why immediately. Social mobility, when great masses of people suddenly, within a brief span of time, change their occupation, dress, and customs, is conducive to imitation. Strong caste divisions used to make imitation difficult (for example, a bourgeois who pretended to be a member of the landed gentry was laughed at). Imitation means close observation of another and the desire to have as much as he has (money, clothes, freedom, etc.). And here is where a personality that spreads terror appears – it exists in every person as the 'I-for-others' that torments the 'I-for-myself.' One can imagine a state in which a person is relatively indifferent to the behavior of others, if only because their station is too high (for example, wearing folk costumes because only city people wear manufactured clothes), or because, at ease with his uniqueness, he calmly tells himself: 'That's not for me.' However, in the twentieth century we have been forced to be ashamed of our particularity. 'I-for-myself' is, after all, always a shame and a sin, although different people will cope with it more or less successfully. When a person is constantly having it drummed into his head that others are enjoying life as they should, he does not stop to think about the illusory character of this image that depicts people from the outside, that is, in such a way that every man is 'I-for-others.' He looks around and starts to be envious: that person over there, he's a miserable creature, and yet look at how much he's received, how many gifts have been showered upon him – he's not below the norm, I am. This 'normality' or 'I-for-others' is, after all, the secret of the diffusion of the 'new ethics,' namely, the characteristic feature of the 'permissive society.' Each of us has a 'calling' that comprises his diversion from the norm, an appeal directed at this and not that individual. The object of envy is not others in the guise of Charles, Peter, or Ignatius, but in the guise of 'normality' as seen from the outside, which we allegedly have too little of. 'Reification,' imitation, and *invidia* are closely interconnected.

But does the desire to become 'the same as everyone else' really indicate that one is envious? So it seems. I don't have what he has, it's owed me, because if I should have it, then I would have a lot more (being myself, my individuality, of course). 'Normality' will be an addition to my individuality, while, in my opinion, the essence of this other person is being dissipated in it.

If we divide envy according to its target – a small group based, for example, on profession, or 'people in general,' the latter would be more dangerous. It is easy to err when we don't want to accept our own destiny, which has been given to us alone, when we are unable to make our peace with the thought that some types of lifestyles are beyond our abilities and would even be painful for us. When we make the effort to conform, various miseries of the 'man in the crowd' reveal themselves to us.

Ira

Bah, if only it were old-fashioned anger that visits us. It is bad to turn purple in the face from fury; even worse to knock someone flat with a blow to the head and kill him in a fit of rage. Even if someone doesn't carry a hatchet around with him, he may well know the belated regrets of a hothead when it's already too late to make amends. But in addition to this age-old anger, a new, modern anger appeared on the scene when we began to feel responsible for evil as members of society and participants in history. Your guts churn, you grit your teeth, clench your fists – but hold your tongue, you are a cipher and can change nothing. And you ask yourself: 'Am I crazy or are they crazy? Maybe it's me, because they go right on living and feel neither indignation nor terror in the face of their own co-responsibility.' If we are born with an inclination to anger, and in this lovely century, to boot, what should we do, how are we to cope? Obviously, each person receives an upbringing; just living among others shapes him. He notices that yelling and banging his head against the wall hardly help; if he is a poet, he becomes convinced that making a lot of noise is not very useful. So his anger goes underground and emerges only in disguise, transformed into irony, sarcasm, or icy calm, from which it is often hard to deduce that fury lies concealed behind it.

I spent my entire conscious life in just such maneuvers with my own anger, never, even to this day, understanding how it could be reconciled with my (truly) asocial nature. How, in fact, are we to understand the coexistence within us of contradictory impulses and habits? All the same, my guts kept churning before 1939 and during the war and after. How is it possible, someone will ask quite justifiably, to compare what is incomparable, historical periods and systems marked by a lesser intensity of evil with those in which evil approached its own paroxysm? Unfortunately, the truth is that every human society is multilayered and multilocational. What offends our moral sense does not occur simultaneously in all strata and in all places. Even where the majority of the population is dying of hunger there are beautiful neighborhoods inhabited by the sated, who listen to good music and are interested in – shall we say? – mathematical logic. One should not imagine that those who have been swallowed by a dragon won't experience moments of perfect contentment. For example, one of my memories of felicity is the day in the summer of 1941 when, after a visit to the peasant writer Józef Morton in Chrobrze near Pinczów (we got there by way of a quaint narrow-gauge track that wound through the grass-covered hills), Jerzy Andrzejewski and I got off the train at a tiny station on the outskirts of Cracow from which we had to walk to the city proper. We stopped at a roadside tavern where, in the garden, a wandering Gypsy band was playing, and then, not quite steady on our feet, we slowly entered the outlying streets, where everything, compared to Warsaw, seemed to be part of another country and another era. The hubbub of voices and the colorfulness of the crowd in the artists' café on Łobzowska Street reminded me of Montparnasse at the height of its glory. The waitress who came over to our table was Jewish, the wife of our colleague, a Warsaw poet. So happiness had not ceased to exist – although ten days later a huge roundup demonstrated how illusory are such oases.

It's not only the multiplicity of strata and locations in human society that acts as a universal law. The intentionality of our attention is another law, so that the mind transforms and shuffles all sorts of 'givens.' Where one person sees an injustice that cries out to heaven for vengeance, another sees nothing; where one person evinces no desire for rebellion, another uses guns and places bombs. My thinking about anger is strongly marked by years spent in America; the two zones of time and space, the European and the American, complement each other. American terrorists are not too different from a certain female poet who was quite popular in the Warsaw cafés at the end of the 1930s. Poland at that time offered many causes for anger, but this poet (from a family of intellectuals) was so loaded with hatred that according to her the system was at fault for everything – for what really ought to have been dismantled and what could not be dismantled in Poland, as well as for everything that is immune to dismantling in every collective life. It was she who wrote the rash line: 'We have exchanged the Russian occupation for a Polish occupation' (as if independent Poland after 1918 was no better than czarist Russia), but she was to suffer too much on account of her rashness for it to be worth reproaching her for this today. Her odious poem deserves to be mentioned, however, because in it our own, familiar, twentieth-century anger turns simultaneously against institutions and against, one suspects, the very existence of anything at all. The young Americans from well-to-do white families, no less disturbed by the fate of blacks in the ghetto than the Russian nihilists were by the fate of the peasants, demonstrate a boundless capacity for pumping themselves up with revolutionary rhetoric, but it would be wrong to treat this lightly. The blatant analogies with Dostoevsky's *The Possessed* are probably based on a deeper level than societal relations – most importantly, perhaps, through the figure of Kirillov, the man who condemns himself to death because, as he says, there is no God but there *ought* to be. Is anger, the mighty demon of our epoch, a Promethean outburst in the name of love of people, or is it a declaration of a grudge against a world that is too unjust for life to be worth living? Both the one and the other, I should think, although their proportions here are unclear.

It is easy to understand the anger of the oppressed, the anger of slaves, particularly if you yourself have lived for several years inside the skin of a subhuman. In my century, however, the anger of the privileged who are ashamed of their privilege was even louder. I am fairly well acquainted with this anger. Though very poor as a young man, I still knew that the couple of zlotys in my pocket was practically a fortune for the majority of people in Poland; furthermore, toward the end of the thirties I earned a lot and was able to act the role of the elegant snob. And then in America I could have served as a (doubtful) argument for the defenders of classic capitalism when they assert that 'the best man wins' in it, for my work was rather appreciated. I admit that I hobnobbed with people like myself in my Berkeley and my California, people who had succeeded. 'We *should* bite the hand that feeds us,' one of them said to me. Perhaps. But if so, always bearing in mind the fact that well-fed, rosy-cheeked people have often gotten entangled in duplicity when they pretended that they were suffering.

Acedia

No one can call this failing simply laziness any longer; whatever it may once have been, nowadays it has returned to its original meaning: terror in the face of emptiness, apathy, depression. It's not isolated hermits, however, who are experiencing its sting, but the masses in their millions. A perfect reactionary would say that for their own good they should have been kept in poverty and illiteracy, so that the whip of elemental necessity would have left them only brief moments for resting but not thinking, so that they could have been protected from the influence of half-baked intellectuals exploiting the printed word. It turned out otherwise, and although the model changes depending on the country and the system, the general outlines remain the same; that is, the average man has appeared who knows how to write, read, use a motorcycle or a car. Who is also unprepared for spiritual effort and subject to the power of the quasi-intellectuals, who stuff his head with counterfeit values.

Let us not yearn for the good old days; they were not good. Certainly, the sacral daily life of the medieval city was not, a figment of the imagination, for it did leave a trace in architecture and in art; but at best it can furnish a clue to the distant future, when after the present transitional phase, an ascending movement will be possible – similar, but of, so to speak, a second degree.

For the present, we are in an era when minds are being defiled, which may be the unavoidable price we pay when many human beings are granted access – not just, as in the past, the narrow stratum of the privileged. Access to what? Not to 'culture' – at best, culture is reminiscent of a tightly locked iron chest for which no one has remembered to supply the key. If we may anticipate access, it will be to the 'independent battles' of the human persona. Steeped in tribal customs, the individual did not need this at one time, but today, everyone is beginning to be a hermit in the Egyptian desert and is subject to the law of selection – either ascending or descending into one kind of *skotstvo* or another, to use the Russian term which, although its literal meaning is 'brutishness,' we are inclined, despite the linguists, to link with Greek *skotos* or 'darkness.'

The chaos of values makes precise distinctions impossible at present, so tributes are rendered to illusory greatnesses that are famous because they represent fashionable tendencies in a colorful and forceful manner. This age is, in addition, an age of monsters – humanity has rarely seen their like – but also, as if for the sake of balance, it has produced not a few figures of gigantic proportions, to whom it is no shame to humbly pay tribute. The mental distance between them and the mechanized man in the crowd is probably greater than that between a medieval theologian and, for example, a member of the coopers' guild. To be precise: this is not a judgment based on the level of education, for many who are Nobel laureates in one field of science do not differ intellectually, apart from their specialty, from their least-educated fellow men. Jacques Maritain used to say that the tone of this era has been set by people with weak heads and sensitive hearts, or people with powerful heads and hard hearts, whereas few people unite a sensitive heart with a powerful head. There is no better example of this than the marketplace in America that governs both the language of words and the language of images. Stupid nobility and ignoble commercial cleverness have become so interconnected that when judging journals, films, books, and television programs in terms of their educational influence, one must simply speak of a mass crime against what is called, inaccurately but not inappropriately, 'human dignity.'

Unfortunately, someone who will not slack off, because he knows that *acedia* (or *unyn'e*) is lying in wait for him, will soon notice that the distance between him and his contemporaries increases with every year, if not every month. One of the characteristics of intellectual work is that the same activities begin to demand less and less time; that is, one develops a capacity for abbreviations, for shortcuts. As a consequence, one loses one's taste for the words and images supplied by the market, whence the not inconsiderable problem of the new aristocracy of refined intellects who, however, as I have already suggested elsewhere, move in a different sphere than half a century ago – then, it was 'avant-garde' literature and art that promised more than it was able to fulfill.

Zealous and diligent by temperament, I have worked hard enough, it would seem, that I ought not reproach myself with *unyn'e*. However, I have not done what I could have and the cause was both a flawed education and states of depression that would render impossible a fruitful resistance to the delusions of my time. Obviously, this does not mean that it would have been better had I decided to put on armor early in life, so that nothing from the twentieth century could infect me, as did one of my acquaintances from my youth, who even at that time was preoccupied exclusively with Plato. That would have been an erroneous and

Czesław Miłosz

sterile choice. Here, *nota bene*, it would be appropriate to cite the storminess of history which is not exactly favorable to better judgment. But only a slothful person will presume to cast responsibility onto something that lies outside him.

There is nothing new about grappling with the nothingness that encircles us; man has been faced with these trials for a millennium. However, never before, it seems, not since the times of Caesar's Rome and Hellenistic civilization, has man been so defenseless. These are the consequences of the scientific revolution broken down into small pieces and acting upon the popular imagination in this form. It is possible that the vast majority of people will submit to such nihilizing pressures and will at best search for consolation in the miraculous elixirs sold by Hindu, Buddhist, or Satanic preachers.

Avaritia

It would seem that from time immemorial there has been nothing more universal and more classic. But although greed for money has always driven people to conquest, to oppression, although it has wiped out many species of animals and threatened the entire planet with the chemical poisoning of the water and air, *avaritia* in the present does not assume only those forms that Dante was familiar with. In those days, this failing always characterized a given, specific individual; today, it is spilling over onto mechanisms that are independent of a specific individual, and this also applies to the other cardinal sins, which seem to elude naming because they are cut off from man. For example, is it a result of greed that an oil company pollutes the ocean with its tankers? If we answer in the affirmative, then we see greed where there is no individual, and therefore neither guilt nor contrition. The directors? But they are acting not as people but as a function of the collective body, which has no other aim than the amassing of profits. They are punished for decisions taken in the name of any goal other than profit. They can, it is true, resign their positions and take up something else; this will not, however, change the actions of the corporate body, which yields only to external force.

The situation of the directors of such a corporation is probably emblematic of what confronts the various, and considerably lower, rungs on the social ladder. This or that Jones or Du Pont quietly dreams of virtue; he would eat grass, drink spring water, wear a sack tied with a piece of string; but while his yearning for the Franciscan ideal may be completely sincere, he has been 'captured,' alas, and there is no turning back.

The new, impersonal varieties of greed could, if necessary, be considered one of the reasons why it has ceased to be a literary theme. *Avaritia* as the sinister passion of the heroes of novels has its own history, which more or less parallels the history of the 'realistic' novel. Defoe, Dickens, Balzac, Zola have successors in the West at the beginning of our century, too, primarily among American writers. In Russia, *srebrolub'e* begins its literary career with Pushkin's *Covetous Knight* and occupies a not inconsiderable position in Dostoevsky's biography (he wanted to win a million at roulette) and in practically all his works. The revolution in novelistic technique that we have witnessed took place at a time when the greedy collective, which is very difficult to describe, was already active alongside the greedy individual. But also the very flight from the realia of life somehow caused the novel to stop speaking about money. And when the human jungle stuns us with its wild growth today, literature, occupied with passive experiences and the individual's impressions, steers away from the vulgar questions: Who makes his living at what? Who is paid for what? It is characteristic that the anger of American intellectuals, who, with rare exceptions, are independent of the publishing market because they live off the universities, overlooks the crux of the matter, that is, the market, and even, on the contrary, strikes out at all limitations on the market's freedom, even though in practice that freedom serves the tradesmen-demoralizers. No doubt a powerful taboo is at work here, one of the most mysterious social thermostats, by force of which revolutionary anger at everything that *avaritia* is responsible for becomes transformed into merchandise, that is, assists that same *avaritia*.

More than other failings, it in particular, but also its absence, refers us to the vague laws of personal predestination. Success and failure, measured in money, do not appear to have an unambiguous link with greed or miserliness, although perhaps the middle groups, those who are called neither to wealth nor to poverty, are the most free of *avaritia*. In this middle group the following principle generally holds true: you will have exactly as much money as you need, but under the condition that you are not particularly anxious about it.

Gula

It is painful to think about all one's great-great-grand-fathers succumbing to gluttony and drunkenness; in general, it is painful to think about the genes that one is carrying around inside oneself. The awareness that one has Slavic genes is depressing enough to make the 'taste for pickled cucumbers and boisterousness' seem as burdensome as irreversible Karma; the consequences of this tendency to feasting cannot be evaded, even if subsequently they are gracefully assigned to various geopolitical causes. A simple calculation of the time spent on feasting and thereby lost to thinking over the course of centuries can explain a lot here. Idyllic feasting may testify to an inability to tolerate the world as it is, to a yearning for a gentler world; at the same time, it is one of the chief motivations of self-contempt, for revulsion at drunks in the street seems to merge with revulsion at one's own behavior in the recent past. Low self-esteem, which, to be sure, is rooted not only in this but also in a collective incapacity (so that only individuals are energetic), leads, in turn, to paranoid reflexes; self-revulsion is extended to 'them,' to whomever, who are guilty of everything. That is why one should also notice more than just the loud talk, stupid bragging, and jabbering in a certain type of feasting. Drunkenness itself is less important than what is revealed by drunkenness. And what is revealed is more or less the same among all peoples, with the addition of a given society's particular characteristics. It's the latter that can be the cause of low self-esteem.

I have tried to avoid the traps set by *gula* with varying degrees of success. I admit that this may be taking my practical sense too far, but I have discovered that one can 'profit from one's enemy'; that is, one can ponder those things that surface whenever we carry things too far. And what comes to the fore are reflexes, whims, resentments, and egotisms too un-flattering for us to enjoy being aware of them.

Luxuria

When talk turns to dissoluteness or licentiousness, everyone pricks up his ears; I should, therefore, discourage such expectations ahead of time. For want of other attractions, above all, the attractions of the writer's art itself, the literati compete with each other nowadays in 'sincerity,' and it would no doubt be possible to introduce a new distinction between high style and low style based on this principle. A self-respecting author will not sink to such methods, from which it follows that *belles lettres* are not worth reading because only a very few writers in that genre stay within the bounds of high style.

Dreams of man as happy and liberated have long stood in opposition to all prohibitions and to the hypocrisy that prefers to forget about the libido's hold over us. But eliminating hypocrisy solves very little. D. H. Lawrence says that Adam and Eve's first sexual act after the Original Sin was no different, physiologically, from what they had done many times before. The difference lay in the fact that now each of them *saw*, that is to say, was conscious of his own body and his partner's body as Other; moreover, each was conscious of the fact that the partner was another consciousness. That is why they experienced shame for the first time, were conscious of their nakedness, and hid before the sight of God. 'Who told you that you are naked?' God asked Adam. D. H. Lawrence sought a restoration; he wanted man to be innocent, as he was *before* he tasted the fruit of the Tree of the Knowledge of Good and Evil. This is not the place to consider to what extent we can succeed at that. That conjunction in the Book of Genesis: a man and a woman, the apple (or consciousness), shame, teaches us that in any event our words will not succeed in inhabiting the Garden of Eden and that the field of literature, or the works of the mind, can be, at best, an area on the border and, therefore, something that exists merely *in proximity* to love and death in their innocently physiological aspect.

There are a number of puzzling aspects to the 'sexual liberation' of the second half of our century. Its vehemence can perhaps be explained as a reaction to the entire nineteenth century, not to the period that directly preceded it, since the years of my youth, for example, were not particularly puritanical. Let us agree that revolutions in mores do not occur rapidly; sometimes it takes decades until the so-called masses embrace a universal standard. However, even if we concede this, 'liberation' is striking in its frenzy, as if it were a 'feast in the time of the plague,' whether because the death that threatens the individual has grown more threatening or because the plague is going to destroy the species. This frenzy has its seat not so much in the glands as in the mind, which is filled with shifting images that constantly bombard it from outside, and that are in turn obedient to the dynamics of their own form; in other words, the dose of vividness has to be increased continually. Such a frenzy cannot stop itself and it may well be that it will destroy itself, resulting in an ominous boredom. But it is also possible that it presages a new revolution, which would be a rather paradoxical result of these yearnings for innocence and normality. Science-fiction writers have already written about such visually-olfactorily-tactilely provoked surrogate discharges.

Beatrice is a powerful symbol in *The Divine Comedy*; that is, she is both a real person and a real idea of platonic love in precisely the same degree, or she is neither the one nor the other, because she appears instead of them, so that they cannot be separated. She also leads Dante to the summit – literally, because she leads him to the mountain of Earthly Paradise and even higher – assuming the leadership where Virgil ends his role; that is, where the natural sorcery of art ends.

The present antagonism toward all asceticism and even the particular fury with which it is mocked are sufficient cause for revealing a certain secret. The Divine Arts of Imagination, as Blake called them, are obedient to Eros' summons but at the same time are ill disposed to or, should we say, envious of the procreative urge. This conflict is an entirely serious one, for the arts demand of those who are faithful to them a constant striving without fulfillment, and whether or not the faithful desire it, the arts impose upon them their own monastic rule. There exist a sufficient number of testimonies to that effect; furthermore, the lives of artists and of people who have had mystical experiences can be cited together here, since the issue is the same. The coloring and expressiveness of all 'visions,' whether in dreams or waking, depend on a number of conditions; one of them is a high threshold of erotic energy. 'Unfulfilled' love, from the Provençal ladies of whom the troubadours sang, and their Florentine sister, Beatrice, to the Romantic biographies, bears witness that the entire dualistic, Platonic tradition, which was revived by the Albigensians, responds to some truth in our nature. Or perhaps not to ours, that is, not to man's in general? Of the two types of totalism, the 'permissive' will be more enduring than the 'prohibitive,' because in the former the arts of the imagination will wither of their own accord.

If Only This Could Be Said

To deny, to believe, and to doubt absolutely – this is for man what running is for a horse.

Pascal

If only this could be said: 'I am a Christian, and my Christianity is such and such.' Surely there are people who are capable of making such a statement, but not everyone has that gift. The power of dispossession, of disinheritance, is so great that language itself draws a boundary line. 'In that dark world, where gods have lost their way' (Theodore Roethke), only the path of negation, the *via negativa*, seems to be accessible. It is worthwhile to ponder the difficulty of labeling one-self a Christian. This difficulty is marked by somewhat different characteristics in each branch of Christianity; to speak of 'Christianity in general' would be to forget about many centuries of history and that we each belong to a particular, more or less preserved, tradition. In my case, the difficulty lies in calling myself a Catholic.

The obstacles I encounter derive from shame. We always experience shame in relation to someone; that is why, instead of dilating on religious concepts, I am obliged to make an effort to picture the faces of people before whom I am ashamed. A milieu which is hostile to religion, which thinks of religion as a relic of a past era, would probably arouse my violent opposition and a manifestation of my own religiosity. I am not dealing with such a milieu, however. Actually, I ought to explain the word *milieu*. What I mean by this is a certain number of people, scattered among various cities and countries, but present in my imagination. When I speak about my time or my era, I refer to events that touch me directly, as well as to what I know from books, films, television, the press; but more reliable knowledge is connected to people, to those whose way of life and thinking is familiar to me, to some extent, thanks to our personal relationships. I call this group 'my contemporaries' under the assumption that they can be considered to be representative of a much more inclusive group, although it would be inappropriate to base any far-reaching generalizations on them.

My contemporaries treat religious faith with respect

and a lively interest, but almost always faith is something held by others that they have rejected for themselves. During the first three quarters of the twentieth century such radical changes took place in the way people lead their lives that customs which were still universal in 1900 have acquired the characteristic of exceptions, and my contemporaries experience these changes both as progress and as a loss about which nothing can be done. Once upon a time, the fundamental events of human existence were consecrated by rituals marking a person's entrance into life, fertility, and death. The birth of a child was followed immediately by his acceptance into the community of the faithful, which meant, among Christians, baptism. Then the child submitted to rites of initiation (First Communion, confirmation studies, the sacrament of confirmation). In the countries where I have spent most of my life, in France and America, the existence of these rites, even of baptism, is becoming more and more problematic. They require a decision by the parents, so they are not perceived as self-evident. One of my contemporaries, Albert Camus, once asked me what I think: Is it not a little indecent that he, an atheist, should be sending his children to First Communion? But a decision in favor of the religious education of children does not offer much help, since the language in which the catechist speaks is countered by the impression the surrounding scientific-technological civilization makes upon the imagination.

The existence of marriage rites, rich in symbolism and providing a sense of the succession of generations, is becoming even more problematic. (The central place of this rite in Polish theater – in Wyspiański's *Wedding*, Gombrowicz's *Marriage*, Mrożek's *Tango* – should give us something to think about.) Increasingly, the institution of marriage is being replaced by simply living together, which has followed upon the sundering of the link between sex and fertility. This is not just a revolution in the area of moral norms; it reaches much deeper, into the very definition of man. If the drive which is innate in man as a physiological being conflicts with the optimum condition that we call a human way of life (sufficient food, good living conditions, women's rights), and therefore has to be cheated with the help of science, then the rest of our firmly held convictions about what is natural behavior and what is unnatural fall by the wayside. This distinction between the natural and the unnatural was based on the harmony of Nature, which enfolded and supported man. Now we are forced to recognize that anti-naturalness defines man's very nature. And yet, isn't a belief in salutary cyclicity inherent in every ritual? Doesn't the

Czesław Miłosz

ancient notion that infertility, whether of a woman's womb or of a sowed field, is a disaster provide negative confirmation of this fact? And isn't every kind of ritual dealt a blow when a species has to oppose the cycles of nature?

My contemporaries generally adhere to the rituals accompanying death, because they have to. Faced with the fact that someone has died, a particular sense of helplessness overwhelms family and friends; something has to be done, but no one knows what. This is a moment when the living gather together and form a community which unites, for the occasion, into a farewell circle. It is possible that the more activity that takes place around the deceased, the easier it is to endure the loss, or that lengthy prayers ease sorrow by virtue of something having been done. Burying someone who was movement and energy is too repulsive and at odds with our humanity for us to accept it without a prescribed form: the more conventional it is, the better, for as long as the deceased takes part in our tradition-sanctioned gestures and words, he remains with us; this dance, as it were, includes him in our rhythm and language – in defiance of that great Other about which the only thing we are able to say is that for us it has no properties. That is why over the course of millennia mourning rituals became richly differentiated into liturgy, the lamentations of professional mourners, the funeral feast. Of course, scientific-technological civilization cannot cope with death, because it has always thought only about the living. Death makes a mockery of it: new refrigerators and flights to other planets – what does the one who is lying here care about them? In the face of death the circle of those saying goodbye senses its own buffoonishness, just like the participants in a 'demonic vaudeville,' to borrow Kirillov's phrase from Dostoevsky's *The Possessed*. Whatever may be the beliefs of those gathered there, they accept a religious funeral with a sense of relief. It frees them from the necessity of an almost impossible improvisation at a time when, at best, one can come up with a moment of silence and the playing of a Mozart recording.

I feel obliged to speak the truth to my contemporaries and I feel ashamed if they take me to be someone whom I am not. In their opinion, a person who 'had faith' is fortunate. They assume that as a result of certain inner experiences he was able to find an answer, while they know only questions. So how can I make a profession of faith in the presence of my fellow human beings? After all, I am one of them, seeking, as they do, the laws of inheritance, and I am just as confused. I have no idea at all how to relate to the rituals of initiation. What form should the catechization of children take? How and when should they be prepared to participate in the Eucharist? I even suspect that in a world that is alien to it, religion is too difficult for a young mind, and that in the best of circumstances it will take on the form of an alternate system in that mind, a system of 'as if,' having no connection with reality. One can imagine a state (let this be science fiction for the moment) in which most of the population is educated from childhood in a mundane, materialistic philosophy, only the highest elite has religion, and the citizens of that country are not allowed to concern themselves with religious problems until they are at least forty years old. Furthermore (let us enlarge upon this), this proscription was introduced not to preserve privilege but, sorrowfully, when it was noticed that despite everyone's desire, the simplest religious ideas were as difficult to comprehend as the highest mathematics and that they had been transformed into a kind of gnosis.

A Catholic ought to know what to think about today's sexual morality and about marriage, shouldn't he? Yet I have no opinion about these matters, and it is not because I am indifferent to them. On the contrary, I believe they are crucial. In this regard, it is important to remember that ideas from the late eighteenth and early nineteenth centuries have triumphed: 'free love' was a slogan uniting atheists and anarchists like William Godwin, apocalyptic prophets like William Blake, and utopian socialists. The particular dialectic tension of the Industrial Revolution in its early stages, of repressive morality and the revolt against it, made their appearance. But that revolt would lead to change only thanks to science, which was developing in a context of repressive morality. Taken together, all of this bears scant resemblance to the eighteenth-century libertinism practiced by dissolute aristocrats and their ladies. It is probably not one of those revolutions of moral tolerance which occur repeatedly in history and which alternated with periods of severity. As a representative of a transitional generation, I cannot assume the role of Cato, since sexual freedom was already accepted by my generation, even if not too openly. At the same time, however, the Catholic upbringing I received imposed a severely repressive morality. This is one reason why I tend to distrust my own judgments. I can say nothing good about repression, which crippled me in some ways and poisoned me with pangs of conscience, so that I am not fit to be a teacher of conservative ethical rules. But at the same time, I ask myself this question. These inhibitions and self-imposed prohibitions, without which monogamous ties are impossible – do they not have a fundamental significance for culture, as a school of discipline? Perhaps the proponents of 'free love' would be quite distraught if they could see that today their sermons seem downright puritanical. I also have nothing to say about the rupture of the link between sex and fertility, other than that it has already happened. The subtle comments of theologians seem dubious to me, and I cannot discern a difference in the methods used since their causal effect is the same: the cunning of the human mind deployed against Nature. Which does not mean that I react to the Pope's exhortations like those progressive Catholics who hear in them only the voice of obscurantism. It is, as I have said, a deeper problem than it seems, and that the church is privately tearing its hair out over this testifies to a sense of responsibility for our entire species at a time when it is undergoing a great mutation.

But what of death? I would say that it has made an especially spectacular appearance in my century and that it is the real heroine of the literature and art which is contemporary with my lifetime. Death has always accompanied us, and word, line, color, sound drew their *raison d'être* from opposition to it; it did not, however, always behave with the same majesty. The *danse macabre* that appears in late medieval painting signified the desire to domesticate death or to become familiar with it through its ubiquitous presence, a friendly partnership, as it were. Death was familiar, well known, took part in feasts, had the right to citizenship in the *cité*. Scientific-technological civilization has no place for death, which is such an embarrassment that it spoils all our calculations, but it turns out that this is not for the best. For death intrudes itself into our thoughts the less we wish to think about it. And so literature and art start referring to it incessantly, transforming themselves into an areligious meditation on death and conducting 'pre-casket somatism,' to borrow a phrase from contemporary Polish poetry.

Here, perhaps, is where I part ways with many people with whom I would like to be in solidarity but cannot be. To put it very simply and bluntly, I must ask if I believe that the four Gospels tell the truth. My answer to this is: 'Yes.' So I believe in an absurdity, that Jesus rose from the dead? Just answer without any of those evasions and artful tricks employed by theologians: 'Yes or no?' I answer: 'Yes,' and by that response I nullify death's omnipotence. If I am mistaken in my faith, I offer it as a challenge to the Spirit of the Earth. He is a powerful enemy; his field is the world as mathematical necessity, and in the face of earthly powers how weak an act of faith in the incarnate God seems to be.

I must add immediately that when thinking about my own death or participating with my contemporaries in a funeral ceremony, I am no different from them and my imagination is rendered powerless just as theirs is: it comes up against a blank wall. It is simply impossible for me to form a spatial conception of Heaven and Hell, and the images suggested by the world of art or the poetry of Dante and Milton are of little help. But the imagination can function only spatially; without space the imagination is like a child who wants to build a palace and has no blocks. So what remains is the covenant, the Word, in which man trusts. Who, however, will inherit life? Those who are predestined to do so. I know that I ought not play the role of a judge, yet I do, prompted by the human need to evaluate. So I divide people; that's right, I divide people – as artists used to when painting the Last Judgment – into those who go to the right and those who go to the left, into the saved and the damned. There are many among both the living and the dead whom I call bright spirits, whom I respect and admire, and so I have no doubt that they belong among the saved. But what about the others, those who are like me? Is it true that we ourselves were guilty of all those falls and internal conflicts that tear us apart, of the evil that stifles the weak impulses of our good will? Where does the responsibility for our illnesses lie – for us, patients in hospitals and psychiatric clinics, whatever our illnesses may be, whether physical or spiritual? My criteria are inadequate; I understand nothing.

My contemporaries, or, at least, those whom I value most highly, strive not to lie to themselves. This obligates me. Alas, two traps lie in wait: hypocrisy and exaltation. A man who derives from his own scrupulous fulfillment of religious prescripts a sense of superiority over others, because they are not as scrupulous, is called a Pharisee. The Church as an institution imposes rules concerning participation in its rites; attendance at Mass and confession are not a matter of the heart's needs but a self-imposed discipline accepted by the faithful. In our new conditions, however, a new temptation is born: the more I resemble my contemporaries who are leaving the Church, the more my decision to comply with these rules takes on the appearance of arbitrariness. I respond with a shrug of my shoulders – 'Well, what of it?' – to all the reservations I come up with, and although I don't want to, I grab myself by the scruff of the neck. Alas, I take pride in being able to do that: a Pharisee. As a matter of fact, I don't really believe in these acts; for me, confession is a purely symbolic test of strength. What will win out – revulsion at the completely senseless activity of confessing imaginary sins or obedience to the prescriptions of our mother *Ecclesia*? In this regard, my attitude comes close to

Lutheran conclusions: Man cannot know his own true evil; all he can do is trust in divine mercy, knowing that the sins he confesses to will almost certainly be nothing but a mask and a disguise. In other words, I am with all those people who have proclaimed their distrust of Nature (it's contaminated) and relied solely on the boundless freedom of the divine act, or Grace. That is why, among all the figures of the twentieth century, my writers were Lev Shestov and Simone Weil. In naming them together, I do not wish to obscure the essential differences between them which arose, first and foremost, from the fact that Shestov struggled against Greek philosophy, whereas Weil was fundamentally a Platonist. Nevertheless, even though she often quarreled with Pascal, she was closest to his thinking, and as for Shestov, he, too, praised Pascal and also Luther. That I was drawn to Shestov and Weil was also a function of their style. It is no accident that their language – Russian in Shestov's case, French in Weil's – is clear, severe, spare, superbly balanced, so that among modern philosophers they are the best writers. In my opinion, this proves that in a period when the sacral is available to us only through negation and repudiation of what is anti-sacral, the self-restraint and intellectual rigor of those two places them on the outermost boundary of the very best style, beyond which verbosity begins.

At one time I was prepared to call these tendencies of mine Protestant. With great relief, since nothing links me intellectually with Anglo-Saxon Protestants, I became convinced that it was only a few old Christian currents which had been labeled heretical after the schism and the Tridentine Council, since the warring sides needed to underline and even to invent their differences. The breathtaking casuistic distinctions developed by Catholics attempting to capture the riddle of free will and grace in Aristotelian-Thomist language do not seem convincing to me, and even Jacques Maritain's attempt to resolve this problem toward the end of his long life smells too much of casuistry. It's the same with predestination. It was part of the teachings of the Church long before Martin Luther appeared (those who are predestined to do so will inherit life), and we have been informed erroneously that this is a distinguishing feature of Protestantism.

Hypocrisy and exaltation: struggling with my two souls, I cannot break free of them. One: passionate, fanatical, unyielding in its attachment to discipline and duty, to the enemy of the world; Manichaean, identifying sex with the work of the Devil. The other: reckless, pagan, sensual, ignoble, perfidious. And how could the ascetic in me, with the clenched jaws, think well of that other me? He could only aim for false sublimations, for deceptive Platonisms, convincing himself that *amore sacro* is his calling, and smothering the thought that I am entirely on the side of *amore profano*, even if I clasp my hands and primly purse my lips like a well-behaved young miss. Those two souls have also led me down some strange byways where it was necessary to establish my own relationship to the community, ranging from a thoroughly patriotic devotion akin to that of the nineteenth-century Philomaths all the way to fits of rage and egotistical indifference, which, of course, forced my disciplined half to adopt various disguises and enact various comedies in relation to myself. Alas, I cannot avoid mentioning those internal altercations; they demonstrate that Saint Francis's cheerfulness is not for me. Although, I must say, one of my old English friends once told me that there is a lot of *gaiety* in me, which is probably true, and means that there is such a thing as a despairing cheerfulness.

Nowadays, we tend to exaggerate the difficulty of having faith; in the past, when religion was a matter of custom, very few people would have been able to say what and how they believed. There existed an intermediary stratum of half-conscious convictions, as it were, supported by trust in the priestly caste. The division of social functions also occurred in the field of religion. 'Ordinary' mortals turned to the priests, setting the terms of an unwritten contract: We will till the soil, go to war, engage in trade, and you will mutter prayers for us, sprinkle holy water, perform pious singing, and preserve in your tomes knowledge about what we must believe in. An important component of the aura that surrounded me in my childhood was the presence of clergy, who were distinguished from those around them by their clothing, and in daily life and in church by their gestures and language. The soutane, the chasuble, the priest's ascending the steps before the altar, his intonations in Latin, in the name of and in lieu of the faithful, created a sense of security, the feeling that there is something in reserve, something to fall back on as a last resort; that they, the priestly caste, do this 'for us.' Men have a strong need for authority, and I believe this need was unusually strong in me; when the clergy took off their priestly robes after Vatican II, I felt that something was lacking. Ritual and theater are ruled by similar laws: we know that the actor dressed up as a king is not a king, or so it would seem, but to a certain extent we believe that he is. The Latin, the shimmering chasubles, the priest's position with his face toward the altar and his back to the faithful, made him an actor in a sacral theater. After Vatican II the clergy shed not only their robes and Latin but also, at least here, where I write this, the language of centuries-old formulas which they had used in their sermons. When, however, they began speaking in the language of newspapers, their lack of intellectual preparation was revealed, along with the weakness of timid, often unprepossessing people who showed deference to 'the world,' which we, the laity, had already had enough of.

The child who dwells inside us trusts that there are wise men somewhere who know the truth. That is the source of the beauty and passion of intellectual pursuits – in philosophical and theological books, in lecture halls. Various 'initiations into mystery' were also said to satisfy that need, be it through the alchemist's workshop or acceptance into a lodge (let us recall Mozart's *Magic Flute*). As we move from youthful enthusiasms to the bitterness of maturity, it becomes ever more difficult to anticipate that we will discover the center of true wisdom, and then one day, suddenly, we realize that others expect to hear dazzling truths from us (literal or figurative) graybeards.

Among Catholics that process was until recently eased by the consciousness that the clergy acted in a dual function: as actors of the sacred theater and as the 'knowledgeable caste,' the bearers of dogmas dispensed, as if from a treasure house, by the center, the Vatican. By democratizing and anarchizing, up to and including the realm of what, it would seem, were the unassailable truths of faith, *aggiornamento* also struck a blow at the 'knowing' function of the clergy. An entirely new and unusual situation arose in which, at least in those places where I was able to observe this, the flock at best tolerates its shepherds, who have very little idea of what to do. Because man is *Homo ritualis*, a search takes place for collectively created Form, but it is obvious that any liturgy (reaching deep into one or another interpretation of dogma) which is elaborated communally, experimentally, can not help but take shape as a relative, interhuman Form.

Perhaps this is how it should be, and these are the incomprehensible paths of the Holy Spirit, the beginning of man's maturity and of a universal priesthood instead of a priesthood of one caste? I do not want this to sound like an admission that the Protestant isolation of individuals is correct, on the basis of which each individual may treat religion as a completely personal matter; this is delusive and leads to unconscious social dependencies. It would be useless for man to try to touch fire with his bare hands; the same is true of the mysterious, sacral dimension of being, which man approaches only through *metaxu*, as Simone Weil calls it, through intermediaries such as fatherland, customs, language. It is true that although

I would characterize my religion as childishly magical, formed on its deepest level by the *metaxu* which surrounded me in my childhood, it was the adhesions of Polishness in Catholicism that later distanced me from the Church. I cannot say how I would react to this today, because I have lived for a long time outside the Polish-speaking religious community. With rare exceptions, for me Catholics are French, Italian, and Irish, and the language of the liturgy is English. In other words, what happened inside me, of necessity, was a division into two spheres, or rather a change in only one of them, since I myself stuck with the Polish language and with everything that this language carries with it. The pain and fits of anger that 'national religion' (i.e., parochialism) provoked in me, and the right-wing political ideology among those who took part in the rituals, remain in my memory, but perhaps they no longer interfere with my looking at these matters from the broader perspective of time. Catholicism, divorced by now from borscht with dumplings and nationalistic programs, seems to me to be the indispensable background for everything that will be truly creative in Polish culture, although I feel that the present moment is preparatory and portends an era of fundamental rethinking.

Though circumstances disconnected me from the community of those praying in Polish, this does not mean that the 'communal' side of Catholicism vanished for me. Quite the contrary; the coming together of a certain number of people to participate in something that exceeds them and unites them is, for me, one of the greatest of marvels, of significant experiences. Even though the majority of those who attend church are elderly (this was true two and three generations ago, too, which means that old age is a vocation, an order which everyone enters in turn), these old people, after all, were young however many years ago and not overly zealous in their practice at that time. It is precisely the frailty, the human infirmity, the ultimate human aloneness seeking to be rescued in the vestibule of the church, in other words, the subject of godless jokes about religion being for old ladies and grandfathers – it is precisely this that affords us transitory moments of heartbreaking empathy and establishes communion between 'Eve's exiles.' Sorrow and wonder intermingle in it, and often it is particularly joyous, as when, for example, fifteen thousand people gather in the underground basilica in Lourdes and together create a thrilling new mass ritual. Not inside the four walls of one's room or in lecture halls or libraries, but through communal participation the veil is parted and for a brief moment the space of Imagination, with a capital *I*, is visible. Such moments allow us to recognize that our imagination is paltry, limited, and that the deliberations of theologians and philosophers are cut to its measure and therefore are completely inadequate for the religion of the Bible. Then complete, true imagination opens like a grand promise and the human privilege of recovery, just as William Blake prophesied.

Ought I to try to explain 'why I believe'? I don't think so. It should suffice if I attempt to convey the coloring or tone. If I believed that man can do good with his own powers, I would have no interest in Christianity. But he cannot, because he is enslaved to his own predatory, domineering instincts, which we may call *proprium*, or self-love, or the Specter. The proposition that even if some good is attainable by man, he does not deserve it, can be proved by experience. Domineering impulses cannot be rooted out, and they often accompany the feeling that one has been chosen to be a passive instrument of the good, that one is gifted with a mission; thus, a mixture of pride and humility, as in Mickiewicz, but also in so many other bards and prophets, which also makes it the motivator of action. This complete human poverty, since even what is most elevated must be supported and nourished by the aggression of the perverse 'I' is, for me, an argument against any and all assumptions of a reliance on the natural order.

Evil grows and bears fruit, which is understandable, because it has logic and probability on its side and also, of course, strength. The resistance of tiny kernels of good, to which no one grants the power of causing far-reaching consequences, is entirely mysterious, however. Such seeming nothingness not only lasts but contains within itself enormous energy which is revealed gradually. One can draw momentous conclusions from this: despite their complete entanglement in earthly causality, human beings have a role in something that could be called superterrestrial causality, and thanks to it they are, potentially, miracle workers. The more harshly we judge human life as a hopeless undertaking and the more we rid ourselves of illusions, the closer we are to the truth, which is cruel. Yet it would be incomplete if we were to overlook the true 'good news,' the news of victory. It may be difficult for young people to attain it. Only the passing of years demonstrates that our own good impulses and those of our contemporaries, even if only short-lived, do not pass without a trace. This, in turn, inclines us to reflect on the hierarchical structure of being. If even creatures so convoluted and imperfect can accomplish something, how much more might creatures greater than they in the strength of their faith and love accomplish? And what about those who are even higher than they are? Divine humanity, the Incarnation, presents itself as the highest rung on this hierarchical ladder. To move mountains with a word is not for us, but this does not mean that it is impossible. Were not Matthew, Mark, Luke, and John miracle workers by virtue of their having written the Gospels?

Anus Mundi

The cloaca of the world. A certain German wrote down that definition of Poland in 1942. I spent the war years there and afterward, for years, I attempted to understand what it means to bear such an experience inside oneself. As is well known, the philosopher Adorno said that it would be an abomination to write lyric poetry after Auschwitz, and the philosopher Emmanuel Levinas gave the year 1941 as the date when God 'abandoned' us. Whereas I wrote idyllic verses, 'The world' and a number of others, in the very center of what was taking place in the *anus mundi*, and not by any means out of ignorance. Do I deserve to be condemned for this? Possibly, it would be just as good to write either a bill of accusation or a defense.

Horror is the law of the world of living creatures, and civilization is concerned with masking that truth. Literature and art refine and beautify, and if they were to depict reality naked, just as everyone suspects it is (although we defend ourselves against that knowledge), no one would be able to stand it. Western Europe can be accused of the deceit of civilization. During the Industrial Revolution it sacrificed human beings to the Baal of progress; then it engaged in trench warfare. A long time ago, I read a manuscript by one Mr Ulrich, who fought at Verdun as a German infantry soldier. Those people were captured like the prisoners in Auschwitz, but the waters of oblivion have closed over their torment and death. The habits of civilization have a certain enduring quality and the Germans in occupied Western Europe were obviously embarrassed and concealed their aims, while in Poland they acted completely openly.

It is entirely human and understandable to be stunned by blatant criminality and to cry out, 'That's impossible!' and yet, it was possible. But those who proclaim that God 'abandoned us in 1941' are acting like conservators of an anodyne civilization. And what about the history of humankind, with its millennia of mutual murder? To say nothing of natural catastrophes, or of the plague, which depopulated Europe in the fourteenth century. Nor of those aspects of human life which do not need a grand public arena to display their subservience to the laws of earth.

Life does not like death. The body, as long as it is able to, sets in opposition to death the heart's contractions and the warmth of circulating blood. Gentle verses written in the midst of horror declare themselves for life; they are the body's rebellion against its destruction. They are *carmina*, or incantations deployed in order that the horror should disappear for a moment and harmony emerge – the harmony of civilization or, what amounts to the same thing, of childish peace. They comfort us, giving us to understand that what takes place in *anus mundi* is transitory, and that harmony is enduring – which is not at all a certainty.

From 'Notebook'

The world was unattainable and there were too many people. I was living in constant naive amazement. And I was uncertain whether by judging the strangeness surrounding me I was resisting the kernel of madness at the heart of human existence and also the features of a particular civilization. Perhaps vitality itself has always forced me, in the end, to choose the other path.

Energy should encounter resistance; resistance keeps it in practice, rescues it. If, however, energy comes up against a gigantic smooth wall on which there is not a single rough place, not even a crack, this is more than resistance; it is too much. Energy then turns inward, consumes itself, and a person asks himself, 'could it be that there is no wall? Could this be my own delusion? Could it be that all this is my own fault and I should adjust to it?'

*

A young mathematics teacher whom I befriended showed me one of his poems. It was a poem about a man who tries in vain to climb out of a dark well. In the end, it turns out that this man is the *son* of the one who built the well.

My fascination with Robinson Jeffers derives from the fact that his assumptions were erroneous and blasphemous. He exemplifies the law of the delayed development of two literatures, American and Russian, which, borrowing problems and motifs from Western Europe, gave them greater sharpness and forcefulness. Thus, Jeffers's universe, in which man is negated by infinitely extended Newtonian space and by time deprived of any human meaning but arranged into a cycle of eternal return, is the universe of all the nineteenth-century martyrs. Jeffers also expressed most completely that misery which on rare occasions bears the name of vigorous individualism.

All right, it's a truism, but still, making one's peace with this is impossible – this idea that millions of people sense that their lives are somehow defective and deprived (although what they are deprived of, they do not know), and when they attempt to express something, all that comes out of their mouths is a stammering of blind hatred and aggression. Then they die, and who would dare to weigh their poor souls on the scales of good and evil?

Perhaps my life was triumphant not because it lacked evil and defeats but because I could see with my own eyes how what was just a vague promise is slowly being fulfilled and how that which I suspected of false greatness is disintegrating. The concealed structure of reality is reasonable. To assert this in this terrifying century is a great deal. Nonetheless, almost never, with the exception of a few brief moments, did the conviction abandon me that sooner or later the absurd will fail, and this is what distinguished me from my despairing contemporaries. Impossible to name, accessible only to intuition, the very fabric of movement seemed to me miraculous.

Art against thought, which has been intercepted, separated from the imagination, sentenced to a meager diet of scientific superstitions, shackled with vulgarization. It may well be that this dilemma of the entire nineteenth century attained its most tragic dimensions in the Russian poets who were born around 1890: Anna Akhmatova, Boris Pasternak, Marina Tsvetaeva. They had nothing but a belief in their own powerful, jealous daimonian, who destroyed their human happiness so that their work could be born; this was their Saint George fighting with the dragon. But the dragon, the same one which defeated Baudelaire and Rimbaud, was even more powerful; it had grown heads and fangs.

Modern artists entertain flattering notions about sin, since virtue is the underpinning of the established social order. In this way they try to forget about the moral contradictions of their profession. Art is born out of the desire for good, but concepts and form demand faith in oneself, which derives from infatuation with the agility of one's own mind. Pride, disdain, arrogance, anger are what support an imperiousness that opposes the whole world. People say that we do not deserve to go to hell, because our work redeems our guilt, but perhaps that is just another sentimental misconception.

Atrocity has always lurked just below the surface of our daily hustle and bustle, our habits, social organizations, phrases, smiles; the war years merely brought it to the surface. Afterward, in some other country, in some other city, I used to pause for a moment in the middle of a teeming crowd and say, 'Stop this finickiness! If it lasts for even this one more day, that will be good enough.'

★

When we deny the existence of God on the grounds that no one who is good could have thought up a world in which living beings are subjected to such tortures, we treat our denial as an action that has the power to change something; in other words, we hope to shame God.

Right after the war, Kazimierz Wyka, trying to find a label for a certain generation, spoke of those who were 'infected with death.' But man forgets, even to the extent that he gradually begins to doubt the reality of what he saw with his own eyes. He knows that this forgetting is vile, yet if he were constantly thinking 'about that,' everything except this one matter would have no meaning for him. That is why ethical poetry and prose arose on that hazy borderline where one is already beginning to forget but one still remembers.

Men and women carry within their imaginations an image of themselves and of others as sexual beings and often that is the only thing that humanizes them. The sexual organs remind us of the transience, the fragility, the insecurity of existence; it is not for nothing that love and death have always been connected. Let us, then, praise guttural intonations, giggles, the lustfulness of eyes. An asexual imagination is the threat of abstraction, mechanical dolls passing each other, an invitation to murder. But the moment when the assembly of men and women appears in their childlike, immature form, with all the sly awkwardness of their evasions, is both possible and necessary. Then the fear of what is referred to as the demonism of sex, that is, of Nature who mocks our values, is tempered by pity and humor, fraternity appears, and a glimmer of paradise lost.

Could it be that another reason why the novel has become impossible is that we are no longer amused by the contrast between behavior prescribed by convention and our corporeality? A hot potato dropping into someone's codpiece during a theological dispute at the dinner table, as in *Tristram Shandy*, is no subject for the demonic inhabitants of the modern city, the *cité infernale*.

We should be grateful for what was given to us in a corner of Europe that was not part of the twentieth, or even the nineteenth, century. We couldn't appreciate it – until later on, observing people who never knew the warmth of organic ties and who try in vain to warm themselves by traveling to the Solomon Islands or to derelict Mexican villages.

Chuckling, I passed by the thick volumes on the library shelves, because on those volumes were the names of people whom I used to know in their corporeality, their vacillations, little games, ridiculous behaviors, downfalls, ravings. But there they were: frozen, preserved, forever. Connected by our *mentalité*, our style (the differences among us are bound to fade), we carved our state in time, a niche or a cavern, which will be overlooked by our immediate heirs and discovered only later, and then evaluated from some new perspective. That was one facet. The other was when I walked around for an hour in a labyrinth of mountain grottoes in Oregon that were discovered by sheer chance at the end of the nineteenth century (a bear that was being hunted suddenly disappeared, 'vanished under the earth,' along with the dogs running after it). The stalactites and stalagmites bored me, but the wonder of nature acted upon me, transforming itself into a humanistic picture, through its connection with the shelves of a library.

Considering the excessive amount of printed paper, perhaps it is time now to introduce a rule limiting articles, essays, and the like to a single sentence?

If I remain silent for a long time, perhaps it is because I have been overwhelmed by a fear known to everyone who, from an excitation of the blood, has risen to acts of courage out of ignorance of the danger involved, and only later broke out in a cold sweat, his teeth chattering?

Why should I not confess to my own stupidity and admit that I have used words to touch upon that which ought not be touched?

Entering the Mission of San José, which was built at the end of the eighteenth century, I knew from the smell of the walls, the old wood, the leather straps, that I had returned home, because where I had spent the happiest years of my childhood, by virtue of provincial wonders, everything had frozen in time in the final years of the old Republic, so how different I was from the other tourists marveling here at a bygone era.

My contemporaries prided themselves on having ceased to persecute artists and writers for being unintelligible, but it never entered their minds that that splendid tolerance referred to yesterday's unintelligibility and that perhaps certain types of simplicity had now become unintelligible to them.

If, despite everything, I would not wish to live in the nineteenth century, because then I would not have the consciousness which I still find difficult to name, but which embraces humanity as a whole, as a unit, as predestination, then let's put an end to this pessimistic chatter about regression or the circle of eternal return.

Since poetry, faced with the setbacks of philosophy, is becoming more and more an organ of knowledge, returning, as it were, to the time of early Greece when there was no other philosophy than poetic philosophy, contemporary graphomania has to assume the appearance of intellectual depth.

In England there is a poet named Philip Larkin, who had the audacity to title his first volume of poetry *The Less Deceived*, not realizing that elegant, genial skepticism is an abomination in poetry, which is possible only as a game in which one bets everything one has.

It is easy to understand why the singer Bob Dylan is so popular among California youth now that I have heard his reply to an interviewer who asked him if he considers himself a poet: 'No, I'm *not even* a philosopher . . .'

A poet's maturation should be evaluated not only on the basis of what he has accomplished, but also on the amount of stupidity he has denied access to himself.

For years I used to think about the indecency of all types of artistry, which, in every country I am familiar with, now or in the past, would have been impossible if the fate of the downtrodden and the humiliated were really felt intensely by others.

The question has been raised in our century how artists could write, compose music, paint pictures knowing that there were concentration camps in their country, but people forget that, for example, charming English Romantic poetry arose in comfortable parishes where the pastor's daughters played the spinet, while in the neighboring industrial city it was normal to see people staggering from hunger or dying in the streets.

Novelists, who once were very concerned with the so-called struggle for existence, have escaped into the regions of deep inner experience, as if it is obvious that their characters have somewhere to live and food to eat, but I find such prose, where no mention is made even of money, to be suspect, and I am grateful to my life experiences for my skepticism.

*

I am experiencing this second half of the twentieth century so intensely – kinetic sculpture, new music, fashions, the streetscapes of great cities, social mores – that I am constantly amazed by the bond which, in theory, must exist between me and a certain young man in Wilno in the 1930s.

Of necessity, we have grown accustomed to the absurdity that surrounds us and that so clearly contradicts common sense; the endurance of systems based on this absurdity has seemed to us incomprehensible, but since once already, during the last war, we became convinced that people are punished for a lack of reason, we asked ourselves if this new proliferation of absurdity foreshadows something, or if, in expecting punishment, we are making the mistake of thinking by analogy.

It would seem that all human beings should fall into each other's arms, crying out that they cannot live, but no cry escapes from their throat and the one thing they are more or less capable of doing is putting words on paper or paint on canvas, knowing full well that so-called literature and art are instead of.

*Contemporary ... Provocative ... Outrageous ...
Prophetic ... Groundbreaking ... Funny ... Disturbing ...
Different ... Moving ... Revolutionary ... Inspiring ...
Subversive ... Life-changing ...*

What makes a modern classic?

At Penguin Classics our mission has always been to make the best
books ever written available to everyone. And that also means
constantly redefining and refreshing exactly what makes a 'classic'.
That's where Modern Classics come in. Since 1961 they have been an
organic, ever-growing and ever-evolving list of books from the last
hundred (or so) years that we believe will continue to be read over and
over again.

They could be books that have inspired political dissent, such as
Animal Farm. Some, like *Lolita* or *A Clockwork Orange*, may have
caused shock and outrage. Many have led to great films, from *In Cold
Blood* to *One Flew Over the Cuckoo's Nest*. They have broken down
barriers – whether social, sexual, or, in the case of *Ulysses*, the
boundaries of language itself. And they might – like *Goldfinger* or
Scoop – just be pure classic escapism. Whatever the reason, Penguin
Modern Classics continue to inspire, entertain and enlighten millions
of readers everywhere.

'No publisher has had more influence on reading habits than Penguin'
Independent

'Penguins provided a crash course in world literature'
Guardian

The best books ever written

PENGUIN 🐧 CLASSICS

SINCE 1946

Find out more at www.penguinclassics.com